GETTING TO THE ROOT OF IT

A Healing Balm of Freedom

Gail E. Dudley

Copyright © 2018 by Gail Dudley

Getting to the Root of It: A Healing Balm of Freedom
by Gail Dudley

Printed in the United States of America

ISBN: 978-0-692-19136-1

All rights reserved. No part of this document may be reproduced or transmitted in any form, by any means (electronic, photocopying, recording, or otherwise) without the written permission of the author.

Unless otherwise indicated, Bible quotations are taken from the Holy Bible, New International Version®, NIV®. Copyright ©1973, 1978, 1984, 2011 by Biblica, Inc.® Used by permission. All rights reserved worldwide.

Scripture marked ESV is taken from the Holy Bible, English Standard Version. ESV® Text Edition: 2016. Copyright © 2001 by Crossway Bibles, a publishing ministry of Good News Publishers.

Scripture marked KJV is taken from the King James Version. Public domain.

Scripture marked NKJV is taken from the New King James Version®. Copyright © 1982 by Thomas Nelson. Used by permission. All rights reserved.

Scripture marked (NLT) is taken from the New Living Translation. Copyright © 1996, 2004, 2015 by Tyndale House Foundation. Used by permission of Tyndale House Publishers, Inc., Carol Stream, Illinois 60188. All rights reserved.

Published by:
Gail Dudley, Highly Recommended Int'l Publishing

Cover by:
Dominiq Dudley

Table of Contents

Introduction v

The Gift of Being Your Authentic Self: My Scholastic Viewpoint 15

Week 1 ~ Day 1 .... **21**

    Day 2 31
    Day 3 33
    Day 4 37
    Day 5 41
    Day 6 43
    Day 7 45

Week 2 ~ Day 8 .... **47**

    Day 9 51
    Day 10 55
    Day 11 63
    Day 12 – 14 67

Week 3 ~ Day 15 .... **69**

    Days 16 and 17 73
    Day 18 77
    Days 19 – 21 79

Week 4 ~ Day 22 .... **81**

    Day 23 85
    Day 24 89
    Day 25 93
    Days 26 – 28 (Friday – Sunday) 95

Week 5 ~ Day 29 99
    Days 30 and 31 103
    Day 32 105
    Days 33 – 35 (Friday – Sunday) 107

Week 6 ~ Day 36 109
    Day 37 111
    Day 38 113
    Day 39 115
    Days 40 – 42 (Friday – Sunday) 117

Week 7 ~ Days 43 – 45 119
    Days 46 - 47 121
    Day 48 123
    Sunday ~ Day 49 – It's a Celebration! 125

"Removal of the Masks" Supplemental Article 127
About the Author 135
Additional Books by Gail Dudley 137

Introduction

The joy of the Lord is our strength!
We are worth it!

I discern a mighty healing in God's daughters. I can see the manifestation of His healing wings waiting to consume us with His special anointing. Now is the time to surrender to His loving care.

Even if you have been struggling, the time is now to receive the healing balm of freedom.

Many of us have been in a place of feeling stuck, wounded, frustrated, and filled with pain. Today, I ask, "Do you want to be well?" Have you been feeling worthless, undervalued, and having a sense of being insignificant, but ready to be equipped, empowered, and encouraged? *Getting to the Root of It: A Healing Balm of Freedom* is for you. This book will create a healing place just for you and assist you in getting to a place where through prayer you can be healed and lose the weight of life.

So many women have deep-seated wounds that keep them trapped in suffering and grief. Women have been yearning for healing, but it seems that no matter where they look, triggers to past pain and trauma bring the grief to life again and women are held captive with recurring emotional shock.

There remains an underrepresented "mission field" to help women be free of their wounds. The good news is that healing is available and it's time for women to be liberated to live whole and free!

It all started on August 24, 2012 when I gathered a group of women and men for a four-hour Getting to the Root of It small-group session. After the feedback from a total of twenty-six people who were in attendance, I knew God was using me for something greater than I was able to see immediately. A few months later I offered a Getting to the Root of It group-coaching session. That session was life changing for the five people in attendance.

A couple months later I offered an additional session and learned that God was doing an amazing work through me to those in attendance. Since that time I have offered the Savvy Transformational Weekends, which included a Getting to the Root of It segment. It was clear it was time for me to do something more by allowing God to use me for His greater works. God was clear that I had been faithful, and He had given me the authority to do even more.

At first I did not quite understand what having His authority really meant, but as the days and weeks and months went by I began to see His power working through me when I finally surrendered to Him. My prayers were different. My life was transforming. I started living in a deeper relationship by being fully present with Jesus. In 2016 God deposited the beginning of this workbook, *Getting to the Root of It*. By February 2017 everything came together and I began offering individual and group sessions for *Getting to the Root of It: A Healing Balm of Freedom*, on an international stage.

> **I was compelled to write this book to assist women and girls deal with the areas where they struggle and begin the process to overcome the strongholds of their lives.**

Getting to the Root of It: A Healing Balm of Freedom is a book for women and girls to help identify areas where they can receive healing and freedom. I was compelled to write this book to assist women and girls deal with the areas where they struggle and begin the process to overcome the strongholds of their lives. This book is not a quick fix, but a process where each woman and girl will become stronger over time. This book will help you to build a stronger inner core and receive strength to rely on the healing hand of Jesus based upon biblical principles throughout your life journey.

Throughout the book, I have included three powerful words, the same words I continued to hear God speak to me on my personal journey that began February 17, 2017. Those words are, "Pray to lose." Pray to lose is where we will be able to get to the root and receive a healing balm of freedom. I can say without a doubt that I have been freed from the chains that held me in bondage. As I continue to pray to lose, I experience the weight of life being released that I had sympathetically held onto in times past. I had believed the lies of the enemy that what was on the surface of my life situations were things I created and accepted as a part of my daily life. I had conveniently forgotten the words of the book *Who Told You That? The Truth about the Lies* that I myself penned a few years ago. God had

Introduction

to remind me that He called me to a ministry of prayer. He needed me to do for myself the very things I do for others.

I needed to pray. I needed to walk in the authority He has given me and speak life and not live in a defeated life situation. God also reminded me of John 14:12, "Very truly I tell you, whoever believes in me will do the works I have been doing, and they will do even greater things than these, because I am going to the Father." I had to access the authority of Jesus, and boldly live out that authority. I had to believe that as a daughter of the King I can do greater works. I had to speak those things that are not as they are (Romans 4:17). When you come across those three little yet powerful words, "Pray to lose," go into a time of prayer and receive a healing balm of freedom.

If you make the commitment, this book, which includes daily worksheets, can set you free. You will have to do the work, but it will truly change your perspective, give you hope, and allow you to live the rest of your life free from the chains that tried to keep you in bondage.

It started for me February 17, 2017 as I was driving to the Jubilee Professional Conference in Pittsburgh, PA. As I was driving during a truly beautiful sunny day I started asking God how to finally break free of past events, pain, and rejection. Clear as day I heard the Holy Spirit say, "Pray to lose." I remember looking around and saying out loud, "What?" Again, I heard "Pray to lose."

It was time for me to receive the healing balm of freedom and lay aside the weight of life by praying to lose the heaviness that was upon my shoulders.

Here's My Story

Releasing the weight is saving my life right now. I am not simply talking about losing body weight. I am talking about an absolute weight transformation from the inside out. Without a doubt, I now see the connection of what we experience on the outside begins on the inside. Can I be real and talk about being wounded? The kind of wound that will suffocate you to your core. For me, my wounds pushed me to eating emotionally. It took a while for me to recognize what was really happening. I was in a spiritual battle that was pushing me to the brink of catastrophe. My mind had become a true battlefield. Yes, I was gaining weight and the body fat was creating an atmosphere that had me in a state of doom and gloom, but it was much deeper than that. I had to first deal with the wounds that had taken place on the inside before I could deal with the outside.

The more I evaluated my own stuff, the more I realized how this fight was something I needed to get to the root of. The battle began the moment I realized I had been avoiding the wounds that placed me in a downward spiral. I had been internalizing my feelings.

I had been carrying around pain, rejection, and wounds, and that is when I started to pack on the weight. I am not simply speaking of adding bad fat cells; I am speaking of the weight of the stress that was weighing me down. I was carrying around the weight of concerns, and wounds that were growing heavier by the day. Have you been there? Can you relate? Losing sleep at night and walking the floors processing what was happening and why.

I was always finding myself asking questions and being disgusted with myself, but never making any headway. I would experience body aches and pains, but never really connected the dots to life and wholeness with the actual stress I was embracing when I needed to truly live for Jesus. I had to come to the knowledge that I had been crippled by a spirit. A wounded spirit whether self-inflicted or ingrained by past life situations that I for some strange reason decided to hold on to.

I needed to get to the root of it. I needed to do the work and see where these actions had taken root for there will come my deliverance.

Through pleading and begging God reminded me of the woman in Luke 13.

> On a Sabbath Jesus was teaching in one of the synagogues, and a woman was there who had been crippled by a spirit for eighteen years. She was bent over and could not straighten up at all. When Jesus saw her, he called her forward and said to her, "Woman, you are set free from your infirmity." Then he put his hands on her, and immediately she straightened up and praised God (Luke 13:10-13).

Why this Scripture? It says, "On a Sabbath Jesus was teaching." This lady had been crippled by a spirit for eighteen years, but that did not stop her from making her way to the synagogue. I believe God reminded me of this woman because she did not throw in the towel. She kept the faith and found her way in the house with Jesus and was healed. She had determination. She had faith. She had value. She had a life to live. Deeper than that she had a love for the Lord that allowed her to stay the course regardless of being bent over, unable to straighten up at all. She was going to hear the teachings of Jesus.

That alone gives me life. It gave me the power to press in to what God was revealing. I may not be physically bent over, unable to straighten up, but because of my wounds my inner spirit was bent over, which created a downcast look on the outside of me. Yes, I could wear masks all day long. For that I gained Academy Awards! But the true self was packing on the pounds from not dealing with the wounds that were mounting on the inside and creating a stronger root that had a grip on me.

I needed to pray. I needed to pray to lose the weight…the weight of life, which resulted in losing the body weight as well.

Introduction

Why Pray?

I started praying…heck…I was begging! I asked God to help me get my weight under control and fast. The more I prayed, the more I realized God had already answered. Honestly, I wasn't buying His answer. I finally gave in once I heard His audible voice say, "Pray to lose."

"Wait! What?" was my initial reply. I asked, "Did you say, "Pray to lose?" With clarity, I heard, "Pray to lose." God made sure to clarify what He meant by showing me the weight of life and not my body weight. Honestly, that did not sit well with me. I wanted to attack these added pounds, but He had other plans. I kept wanting to make it about my physical weight, but God wanted me to see that He needed me to deal with my whole self. God wanted me to deal with the unforgiveness, the stress, the past rejections and wounds. For me, I didn't have time for that process. I had wanted to focus my prayers of having these fat cells disappear. However, it was deeper than that for me. I had to get to the root of it by laying aside the weight that hindered my forward motion. I had to throw off everything that was not of God and so easily entangled me. I needed to deal with my mind-set, my emotions, and run with perseverance the race designed just for me (Hebrews 12:1).

> Each morning I prayed specifically for my emotional, mental, physical, and spiritual health, and each morning God gave me instructions. Immediately I noticed the change in my mind-set.

I accepted the call to get to the root and made the commitment to doing exactly as God had instructed. Each morning I prayed specifically for my emotional, mental, physical, and spiritual health, and each morning God gave me instructions. Immediately I noticed the change in my mind-set. As my thought process shifted and the weight of life decreased, so did my physical weight. Within the first week, I had mental clarity, I dropped a few pounds, and inches also decreased. My energy level was at an all-time high, and I found myself sleeping better at night. I felt the transformation taking place. The added benefit was that my jeans no longer fit. They were too big. My bra straps started falling off my shoulders. It is not a miracle; it is that I decided to be obedient and pray holistically.

I wish I could say that life was easy from that moment on, but it was not. It is a struggle, but you must make the decision that when you have a bad day, week, or month that you stay the course. You find the strength to pick up where you left off. I'm not trying to hand you a simple plan of action. I refuse to lie and say it's going to be easy. No! It will not. Yes, Jesus can call you forward, touch you, and immediately you can be healed. Yes, that can happen. The question is, what will you learn from God doing so? How will you be able to handle the next time you are wounded or struck with pain from a loved one? It begins with a relationship with Jesus. A true, intimate, love relationship. It is about trusting God with your life, which includes your pain and struggles. It is about digging deeper and finding the triggers that set you off to begin with. You will be pulling back the layers of avoidance.

> Can you imagine the freedom you are about to experience? A kind of freedom that will thrust you into a new life of living?

You will experience pain as you dive into the root cause of your wounds, but it will be worth it. Can you imagine the freedom you are about to experience? A kind of freedom that will thrust you into a new life of living? WOW! I can't wait for you to experience all God has for you. You are about to release the weight of life for wellness transformation.

God has allowed me to journey for all of 2017 to see the manifestation of the Lord on my life. I am not simply writing words on paper for you to read. I am giving you my experience and I am being completely vulnerable to do so. It's worth it to me to expose myself so that you too may be free. I have been called for such a time as this to share this particular prayer strategy with you, and to help you get to the root of it.

Get ready for the most productive 49 days of your life! Grow deeper in your conversation with God and live the life God has ordained just for you.

> For you formed my inward parts; you knitted me together in my mother's womb. I praise you, for I am fearfully and wonderfully made. Wonderful are your works; my soul knows it very well. My frame was not hidden from you, when I was being made in secret, intricately woven in the depths of the earth (Psalm 139:13-15, ESV).

Getting to the Root of It: A Healing Balm of Freedom is about holistic health. This is about our relationship with Jesus. Our weight of life has everything to do with each area we will focus on during the 49 days.

Here's some of what will be covered in *Getting to the Root of It: A Healing Balm of Freedom*.

- Alignment with God
- Dealing with self-negativity

Introduction

- Prayer. Prayer. And more prayer
- Completing a faith portrait
- Fasting
- Removal of the masks
- Dealing with addictions
- The importance of keeping a journal
- The importance of water
- Mind-set cleanse
- Laughter and chocolate
- 3 Cs: Critical, Comparing, Controlling spirits
- ...and so much more!

Getting to the Root of It: A Healing Balm of Freedom is about experiencing the abundant life. This is a fruitful journey.

There is so much more than losing weight... This is your LIFE! On this journey, God will help you release the weight, stress, worry, concerns, burdens, wounds, etc.

Getting to the Root of It: A Healing Balm of Freedom is the transformational plan to help you become aware of everything you do on this journey and beyond the 49 days. This journey will allow you to identify triggers. This transformational plan gives you a road map that will help you connect all the dots. It's a realistic journey that will be life altering. **Mind. Body. Soul. Spirit.**

Here's the plan.

1. Establish the foundation: With God being the foundation, start each day with prayer and reading Scripture. Without God leading us, we will slow our process, and fail. Without God we can do nothing but fail.

Scripture: John 15:5 NIV

I am the vine; you are the branches. If you remain in me and I in you, you will bear much fruit; apart from me you can do nothing.

- It is important for you to set a goal for yourself. What do you want to have accomplished by Day 49? Be realistic. Pray and ask God what it is He has specifically for you over the next 49 days.
  - o An example of a goal I had: I sought to gain a greater understanding of my self-worth in the eyes of Christ. I also challenged myself to dismiss anything that becomes a roadblock to my forward motion.

_____
_____
_____
_____
_____
_____
_____
_____
_____
_____
_____
_____
_____

2. Lay the foundation:

    - First, admit something is wrong. This journey begins when you are honest enough to admit to yourself that something is wrong. Deal with the fact that you have been wounded. It is our choice to own the wound or avoid it. At some point we have to say, "Okay, I've been wounded. Now what am I going to do about it?" Once we decide to own our wound, then and only then can we participate in the fullness of the life God has for us as leaders.
    - Second, realize that apart from Jesus you may find yourself in a web of deception. No matter what we try to do on our own to get through our place of being wounded, we must seek God, the author and the finisher of our faith, and His will in dealing with the wound.
    - Third, believe God. Not simply believe in God but believe *Him*. No matter how dark the circumstance or disabling the pain, with God there is a way to wholeness and healing.
    - Fourth, we must allow the Holy Spirit to be our guide. It's about being Christ-centered and not self-centered. Ask the Holy Spirit to walk you through the process of healing by dealing with the source of your pain. This is beyond what you feel. This position will allow you to receive from the Lord. You may not like what you see, but it's necessary to get through your wound to a place of healing.
    - Fifth, express your honest feelings to Jesus. It's time to lament! "God, why? How long? Why are people doing this to me?" Tell God, "I've done everything You called me to do! I've been obedient! I've been faithful! What did I do wrong?" Lamenting is good. This helps moves you from your wound to your healing.

Introduction

- Finally, forgive. Forgiveness is necessary. This involves a certain degree of risk. Forgiveness is not forgetting, and it is not excusing, but it is, however, setting you free from the prison you have built around yourself. Failing to forgive — and that includes forgiving yourself — will lead to personal torment.

This may be a difficult road to travel, however, you can begin your journey of healing that may have been damaging to you, family, and ministry, and maybe to your relationship with Christ.

Adapted with permission from Healing Care Ministries, Dr. Terry Wardle

3. Each morning, pray specifically for your holistic well-being. Implement what I have titled 'The Three Ss' into each day:

   1) Spend time in silence and listen to what God is speaking to you specifically,
   2) Study to show yourself approved (2 Timothy 2:15 KJV), and
   3) Share with someone how you are growing. This means praying about having an accountability partner.

4. Keep a journal just for this journey. Pray first then write down exactly what God says. Trust me. He will speak clearly.

   Entry from my journal on February 23, 2017, my Day 7:

   Morning: Examine your lifestyle. Gail, it's about what is in your heart. It's important that I listen to my heart. Philippians 4:8: "…whatever is true, whatever is noble, whatever is right, whatever is pure, whatever is lovely, whatever is admirable — if anything is excellent or praiseworthy — think about such things."

   Evening: God showed me several times I needed to check on my heart. I had anger. I had some sorrow. I had some joy. Then God directed me to pray for the anger, the sorrow, and to celebrate the joy.

5. It is important to do exactly whatever God speaks to you throughout each day.

6. Although this is not solely about body weight, be sure to pray before you eat. Pray before you cook. Pray before you go through the fast-food line. Pray before you exercise. Pray before a meeting. Pray before whatever you do each and every day. The prayer can be as simple as, "God, lead me." Pray early morning. Take time to be present with God asking Him to order your steps. Surrender your day to God. Pray, "Not my will, Lord, but Thy will be done in me and with me today."

7. Check your daily thought process. It's not that your thoughts need changing, but realigned. For example: Eating pizza is not bad. Pray about the pizza you are eating. Don't look at it as bad. Look at it as a choice.

I honestly thought I had lost my mind until I started noticing a change in my life on the third day. I mean an overall change in me.

This Bible study will take you one day at a time over 49 days (7 weeks). Before you turn another page allow me to say, I am not a licensed counselor, dietitian, physician, psychologist, or nutritionist. I am one called by God to implement prayer strategies. *Getting to the Root of It: A Healing Balm of Freedom* is a proven prayer strategy that works. Pray to lose the weight of life is that strategy.

Let's get started! Let's start by offering ourselves the Gift of Being Your Authentic Self. Ready?

The Gift of Being Your Authentic Self: My Scholastic Viewpoint

It has taken me over fifty years to learn the value of self-discovery. So often our natural tendency is to resist vulnerability. However, at a certain point in your life you realize that to finish well, self-discovery is needed. Who are you, really? Difficult question to answer in my earlier years, and I will be honest and share that the journey has not been easy.

I can describe myself in many ways as an African-American, entrepreneur, publisher, writer, speaker, woman, wife, and mother, yet all of those descriptors do not make any sense unless I know myself at the deepest levels of my being. At times I have found myself vacillating up and down the continuum between the joys of life situations to the pain of deep wounds. There have been times where I have felt as if someone were suffocating me in order to keep me from the freedom that was right in front of me. No matter how much I would work to break free by examining my life in a deeper way, inevitably someone would pick at my wounds the moment I could see freedom. Each day, month, and year I grew stronger.

Since examining my life in a deeper way, I have experienced many doors opening along this new journey. I am at the height where no one can stop me or have the opportunity to shake me to my core. It is truly amazing to look back and see where I have been and how I was stuck to where I am now since my authentic self-discovery. Why is knowing yourself so important? What is the best way to know yourself in a deeper way?

One of the ways I discovered is by simply being transparent. We cover up who we are by giving in to other people's expectations. But transparency is pulling back the layers.

Transparency. Vulnerability. Authenticity. Can these layers be pulled back without pain of overexposure? Is there a fear of revealing true self that would allow others the opportunity to cause more pain? If we look back to the beginning to the day we were born, stereotypes and labels appear the moment the doctor yells, "It's a girl!" Within moments parents begin to plot and to plan the life journey of another human being. By the first day of kindergarten we get to explore a major life decision early by responding to the question, "What do you want to be when you grow up?" Doctor? Lawyer? Banker? But how often are we given a choice to say, "I just want to be me"?

Being true to oneself is one of our most difficult endeavors, especially when we all are constantly being prodded to be someone else and others intentionally or unconsciously seek to impose upon us a label of who we should be or what we should do. Yet, once we have grown sufficiently into a deeper understanding of ourselves, we are able to embrace ourselves more fully and live within the uniqueness God has personally designed for us. Here it is increasingly more difficult to give up or compromise our true selves. Being true to our authentic self is both freeing and something that greatly pleases God and we can no longer assume the identity of another.

> Once we have grown sufficiently into a deeper understanding of ourselves, we are able to embrace ourselves more fully and live within the uniqueness God has personally designed for us.

David Benner notes, "Christian spirituality involves a transformation of the self that occurs only when God and self are both deeply known. Both, therefore, have an important place in Christian spirituality."[1] It is true that in order to have a true knowledge of oneself, one must seek a deeper understanding of who God is. Much more than a mere superficial glance, a deeper understanding of God is a consequence of our direct connection to God. Being in His presence and recognizing when He is drawing us closer helps us to look in the mirror to gain an authentic evaluation of ourselves.

It is acknowledging our faults without guilt or shame. It is taking a stand without compromising our identity in Christ when others might try to force us to lay aside the Christ within. There is also a point of transformation that one must experience to get a true understanding of who Christ is. From birth onward individuals search for their true identity. We may start out on one path and one direction only to encounter detours along the way and find that we are approaching an altogether new journey. Tastes change, appearances may change, skills increase with experience, relationships change, career paths change course, and desires and thought patterns may change.

---

[1] David G. Benner, *The Gift of Being Yourself: A Sacred Call to Self-Discovery* (Downers Grove: InterVarsity Press, 2004), 20.

Looking briefly at Hannah in Scripture we find a woman and wife who had a gift of intercession, but for years had been distracted and to some degree oppressed by fantasizing over the life of another. It is easy to focus on a neighbor's gift, life success, and family background and miss the amazing beauty God has ordained specifically for you. Transformation is continuous. One may never be fully transformed until they meet their appointed end of life. It is when we can embrace the complexities of life where we are able to see maturity. It goes beyond everyday changes to making oneself available, but to surrender self in order to gain Christ.

Inasmuch as we look to others for inspiration, one must look within themselves for the greatest gift of all: Jesus. However, if a person is battling low self-esteem or feelings of insignificance, he or she is unable to fully grasp the beauty of who God created us to be. On one hand we are grateful to God for allowing us to be who we desire to be, but on the other hand we are disappointed that we may not have certain gifts and talents of the people around us.

Essentially, we express to God, "I do not like who You created me to be." One could argue that Hannah was complaining about not having children, although her husband Elkanah loved her more than having ten sons. However, others could argue that Hannah had great pain because she was barren and wanted deeply to be able to birth a child for her husband.

Hannah decided to make a decision to stand up, which led her to a place of pouring out her heart and asking God to look in her heart. Hannah was loved. However, Hannah had to get to a place of loving herself. She must have had a trust with God that allowed her to get to the place of exposing her heart. Because of her expression, God answered her request. It is easy to sit back and ask the question, "What changed?" One could argue Hannah crying out through prayer to God allowed her to experience self-love.

If we were to be completely vulnerable we would admit that often we wrestle with the question, "Do I believe God?" Not merely speaking of believing in God, but to believe God and taking Him at His Word. Benner also writes of the blessing of knowing oneself as deeply loved.[2] Because of a lack of knowledge and self-awareness, individuals often have difficulty in loving themselves. We fail to comprehend to whom we truly belong. People live their lives daydreaming about becoming someone without taking a hold of who God created us to be.

Many have lost their true identity by emulating others, hoping to achieve what another may have, without considering the pain we cause God by not accepting that He is the

---

[2] Benner, *The Gift of Being Yourself: A Sacred Call to Self-Discovery*, 48-52.

one who created us for His Kingdom. Transformation begins with a self-evaluation. For me, when I consider my life with twists and turns along with past wounds, it reminds me of the flower beds in my front yard. Year after year we commence with the cleaning of our flower beds. Once while clearing out the weeds I began thinking about my life. Continuously I am amazed at the growth of the weeds. In one particular flower bed the weeds were beginning to look like a forest. This particular day I could see a move of God speaking to me about my life.

I remember vividly while clearing the weeds an extremely tall weed stood strong and unmovable. After a time of spraying and pulling the weeds I decided to get a shovel and begin to dig down deep, forcing the shovel to the root. To my surprise there sat a large rock. Around this rock were roots from the weeds that were thick and were wrapped multiple times around the rock. The thickness of the roots of the weeds allowed the weeds to continue to come back each year with force. Cleaning the beds on the surface causes one to focus only on the beauty that can be seen initially, however, this cleaning is only temporary. It is not until we get to the root of the issue that one can see real transformation.

There are weeds that continue to return because we have not fully dealt with the root causes. In our rushed society, we make excuses when it comes to balance and serenity. We push ourselves to a point where exhaustion takes over, and with increasing responsibility and added burden due to the choices we make. We would rather take care of it ourselves instead of delegating so that we would not have to worry if the assignment is completed.

I have found areas in my life that are neglected due to how I have prioritized, and pressing matters become forgotten and later cause more worry and anxiety. It would be easy to make this argument and blame others, however, I must wrestle with the root cause of having to take control. What is it about us that we are afraid to invite others to come alongside? Benner asks his readers a life-altering question, "How does God feel about you?"[3] My answer today comes from a place of transparency, vulnerability, and authenticity as I seek God for gaining a greater understanding of who I am as His Child and how I may have caused Him tears by trying to be someone He did not call me to be.

Reflecting on my first day of kindergarten when I stood before the class to answer the question, "What do you want to be when you grow up?" I remember yelling out with joy, "I want to help people!" This response caused my parents to come to the school for a parent meeting because I refused to answer as my teacher thought I should have answered: that I wanted to be a secretary. I will never forget crying and yelling, "No, I want to help people." Although my teacher posted on the blackboard my dream was to be a secretary, I never left the thought of wanting to help people.

---

[3] Benner, 48.

The principle of deeply loving oneself will remind me of this time and will propel me forward by taking hold of my five-year-old self who is now over fifty. Secondly, getting to the root and loving my authentic self has allowed me to come from behind the curtain that had me in hiding for many years. Oftentimes I hide my gifts for fear of being rejected. As a woman, I am faced with competition from other females. I have found myself rejected by males as well because of my gifts. I love to write and share stories, though I am very conscious of my shortcomings. For the longest time I allowed my weakness to silence my gift of creating and telling stories that bring life to others.

Because I have been able to get to the root of my own insecurities, I have made it a point to ask better questions and take better notes along the way. I am able to admit my weakness and find a way to press forward, realizing that each time I write a story, an article, or a paper, I hold on to my authentic self. I realize that I refuse to stay where I used to be and grow to the place where I want to be. I have now embraced that my weakness will not destroy me or stop me from reaching for my dreams.

> **Coming face-to-face with who I am in God's eyes will allow me to propel forward into all He has for me.**

Coming face-to-face with who I am in God's eyes will allow me to propel forward into all He has for me. So often I have asked for a door to be opened based upon what I have seen others receive. After taking the time to sit with God and do an honest self-evaluation, I realize that I am missing the door God has specifically for me. Hiding behind the curtain and afraid that I may appear insignificant may have caused my delay in accomplishing a broader ministry. That ends here. Now that I have discovered the root of one of my wounds I can avail myself to the transformation process. It is your turn. It is time to get to the root of it.

> Reflection question for me: How have I lived out my authentic self?
> Reflection question for you: How have you lived out your authentic self?

Dear heavenly Father, thank You for Your hand of healing and protection. We come to You fully surrendered. Heavenly Father, Your Word says in Jeremiah 33 to call upon You and You will answer us and tell us great and unsearchable thing we do not know or understand. Today we cry out asking You to show us great and mighty things. Give us a glimpse of Your love in this season of our lives. Thank You for giving us the strength to clean the weeds from our lives down to the root.

Thank You for leading us to our greater purpose. Lord, give us strength to come from behind the curtain and press through our fears, and live a life worthy of the calling You have for us individually and collectively. Lord, we petition You by praying, "Oh, that You would bless us indeed, and enlarge our territory, that Your hand would be with us, and that You would keep us from evil, that we may not cause pain to ourselves or to others." Lord, we ask that You grant to us what we have prayed the way You granted this same request to Jabez according to 1 Chronicles 4:9-10. In the name of Jesus, we pray. Amen.

Describe your authentic self. Write out your true story. Don't worry. No one will read your story but you. This is the beginning of the rest of your life. It's time to get to the root of it and be completely free.

_____
_____
_____
_____
_____
_____
_____
_____
_____
_____
_____
_____
_____
_____
_____
_____
_____
_____
_____
_____
_____
_____
_____
_____
_____
_____
_____

Week 1 ~ Day 1

(Monday) This study is set to begin on a Monday. It is important to begin your 49 days on a Monday.

It's time to wake up!

> Awake, awake, Zion,
> clothe yourself with strength!
> Put on your garments of splendor,
> Jerusalem, the holy city.
> The uncircumcised and defiled
> will not enter you again.
> Shake off your dust;
> rise up, sit enthroned, Jerusalem.
> Free yourself from the chains on your neck,
> Daughter Zion, now a captive.
> For this is what the Lord says:
> "You were sold for nothing,
> and without money you will be redeemed (Isaiah 52:1-3)

Ever had the experience where you cannot seem to see the light of day, but for some reason you keep pressing forward, praying for the day for God to arrive and set you free?

We have prayed. We have cried. We have lamented over our life situations.

Some of us may have given in to the pressure of life and found ourselves mimicking someone else's walk of life in hopes that it would bring us greater joy, and yet it has taken us into a deeper depression.

We are reading God's Word, tuning in to every Christian broadcast available, and attending every conference listed, hoping to get free from pain, and yet many of us still find ourselves in a great depression or in a state of fluctuation.

This oppression, depression, confusion, and uncertainty have become a way of living that we cannot even wrap our minds around—the thought to live our lives dangerously *(in a good way)* for fear that we will once again experience rejection, torment, or some sort of abuse by our oppressors. So many are stuck. This mess has become a way of life and we find it impossible to grab a hold of anything meaningful or good in our lives.

We find ourselves in the darkness of life, barely able to grasp a breath without the loud beating of our heart, that if we are not careful we may find ourselves passed out on the floor wishing to never rise again. As women, wives, and mothers, we at times appear to be helpless, undetermined, hopeless, and restless.

Wake up!

God is calling us to arise…shake off the dust, free ourselves from the chains, and live in the abundance of all God has for us. We have spent time in prayer seeking God for directions and instruction, and now it is time to wake up and live life into our authentic, proclaimed selves whom God has called us to.

Awake! Awake! This is the clarion call of God!

A call that is clear, urgent, and loud. A call that will shake the very foundation on which you stand. A call to act with haste and without hesitation.

Get up out of your delusional state of defeat and embrace the life God has orchestrated just for you! God is telling us to get up out of our slump and by grace present ourselves as a living sacrifice, holy and acceptable unto Him, as He alone presents us to the world, displaying His power and glory!

Jerusalem was to awake not only because her exile was ending, but also because she would be freshly adorned with new clothes, that is, she would be rebuilt.

God is telling us as He told Jerusalem to wake up! Why?

Because He is doing something new! Our season of calamity has come to an end.

The time of judgment is over!

It's like living in financial debt, and the desire to be free. However, we stay in debt because we are still lingering to the past and trying to live up to the standards of what others expect from us and not what God desires from us.

Week 1 ~ Day 1

Imagine all the stuff you have. Things you really don't need or really want. It was something to buy because it felt good. Yes, meaning you were nursing a wound by going shopping for things that you really could not afford. What you really desire is a better, different way of living your life, but you were going about it all wrong because it was only a temporary fix. You thought if you purchased that new pair of shoes or that new car you would feel better…life would be different. That's temporary.

You still did not take the time to deal with the wound by getting to the root of the problem. You were fixing the outside with the hopes of changing the inside and it didn't work. You actually added more stress because you have a mountain of unnecessary debt that is weighing you down. You do know the stress can also cause a weight problem. Here's the truth. Studies show that one is more likely to purchase high-end goods and consume foods high in calories when we begin to feed our mind with self-deprecating thoughts.

> It's time to change the intoxicating thoughts and be free from the wounds, pain, and rejection.

Getting to the Root of It will help break that cycle. It's time to change the intoxicating thoughts and be free from the wounds, pain, and rejection. Just like any cycle of debt and overspending craziness you may have experienced in your life. Worry, food, and financial challenges are all tied into life and the way we choose to live. If we get to the root of it, we will experience a shift in our mind-set.

Again, I say, "The time of judgment is over!"

It is time for you to truly discover who you are in this season of your life. You are the main character of your story. Pray. Pay attention. Put on your garments. This is not one size fits all. For you are fearfully and wonderfully made (Psalm 139:14).

Listen to what God is speaking specifically to you. In order to do so you must shut out all of the noise. This means stop asking others what to do when God is already speaking to you. Stop ignoring Jesus and be obedient to His instructions. Close out all of the distractions. This will position you to live in the overflow as you lean in to Jesus.

Express yourself to Jesus. Start living out who you desire to be. God has already ordained you and called you into this season. Live as He and He alone has called you to live. Stop walking in fear. Stop being afraid of what others may say. What worked for them will not work for you because you are different. It is time to get to the root of it and live for God without the chains around your neck. The Scripture says, "Shake off the dust…free yourself from the chains around your neck." This tells me that we have the power to do just that. Shake off the old stuff and be free from the limitations you have set on yourself.

Make a decision to live! This is personal. We must arise from our low state of being. It is time to start feeling again and free ourselves from numbness and our drowsy condition. It is time to get to the root of it! Yes, challenges will come. We have been in a state of despair far too long that we may find it difficult to truly be free and live because of the natural sense to continue to operate from a place of our woundedness.

This is like the flower bed I shared earlier in the introduction of this Bible study. We have a tendency to clean the surface without getting to the root of the problem. When this happens, the roots grow stronger and force us to work harder. This is not a one-time fix. This is a process. It becomes a morning affirmation so to speak. We have to continue to shake off the dust and free ourselves from the chains around our necks. Each day we must visualize these steps. When you get out of your bed, had your morning coffee or tea, and your shower…pray and then:

1) Clothe yourself with strength by putting on the power of God.

2) Remove the garment of sorrow and heaviness and allow yourself space to refresh and be revived. Live in joy and gladness.

3) Adorn yourself by receiving God's strength. This may be a point of contention for you. You may have experienced deep-rooted rejection and been filled with lies. These things have weighed you down with grief and sorrow. However, today, you can prepare for a joyful and prosperous condition. When you put on that necklace or belt, imagine putting on God's strength.

4) Put on your garments of splendor. It's not singular. The word splendor exemplifies magnificent appearance and grandeur. Take your time. We are becoming healthy one step at a time. Therefore, we must dress accordingly.

5) Assume confidence! Tell yourself, *"I can do all things through Christ who strengthens me"* (Philippians 4:13, NKJV).

Let's pause right here for a moment and digest the first five points. What are you thinking? How will you incorporate this into your daily life?

_____
_____
_____
_____

Week 1 ~ Day 1

_____
_____
_____
_____
_____

Write a quick prayer of focus as you press forward.

_____
_____
_____
_____
_____

6) Shake off your dust. Stop mourning what you have lost when it comes to past rejection, pain, and wounds. Shake it off! Have you ever sat by the window when the sun was shining and looked around the baseboards of your home or looked at the bookshelves and saw nothing but dust? This is what your situation may look like because you are mourning over your wounds. Time to release those wounds by shaking off the dust.

7) Free yourself from the chains on your neck. They are choking you. You're killing yourself with a slow death because of the chains around your neck. Think about a chokehold. It is a tight grip around a person's neck that is used to restrain a person by restricting breathing. These chains around your neck are interfering with your regular breathing. These chains are preventing air to flow and it is stopping the blood from passing through to open your passageway. Having the lack of blood or airflow may lead you to pass out to a state of unconsciousness, which could also lead to death. This is what happens when we go into a state of isolation.

> "Isolation leads to darkness. Darkness leads to secrets. Secrets lead to sickness; and sickness can lead to spiritual death."
>
> ~ Gail Dudley

It is time to live. It is time to be free, never again to be enslaved by the weight of life.

8) Sit up straight. Roll those shoulders back. Lift your head up. Roll out of bed. Open the curtains and blinds. Put on some music and dance. It is a new day!

It is redemption time! "…and without money you will be redeemed" (Isaiah 52:3).

Jerusalem had been **sold** because of her sins, but now she would **be redeemed**, which is to be purchased out of slavery. God is ready to bring you into your new season without having to pay one penny. He paid it all on the cross. You are priceless! You are that important to Jesus.

So here we are. We are fully into Day 1. From here on out there will be daily prompters, Scriptures, prayer guides, and worksheets. This is for you. To get a hundredfold you must do the work.

Days 1 through 7 are set aside for prayer. The first seven days are to take time for silence, get reacquainted with God, and to avail yourself to His voice. We are reawakening to the voice of Jesus and sensing His presence.

Let's pray.

I encourage you to come out of your comfort zone and try a different prayer position each day as indicated in this Bible study. Each prayer position can be used for prayer; however, each position has special meaning for different kinds of prayer…

- Standing with hands raised ~ typical of praise, celebrative prayer, and thanksgiving
- Kneeling and prostration ~ show humility and recognition of a superior
- Slow walking ~ meditational prayer and for quieting yourself. Walking back and forth ~ taking back territory
- Standing ~ act of worship

Prayer is done with your whole self. Our purpose is to have a living response with God, speaking and listening. Pray to lose.

What is your specific prayer request for these first seven days?

_____
_____
_____
_____
_____
_____
_____
_____
_____

Week 1 ~ Day 1

What is your specific prayer request for the seven weeks?

_____
_____
_____
_____
_____
_____
_____
_____
_____

Visualize what you see at the end of the seven weeks and write it here.

_____
_____
_____
_____
_____
_____
_____
_____

Prayer Position is kneeling.

Scripture: 1 Kings 8:54 (KJV)

> And it was so, that when Solomon had made an end of praying all this prayer and supplication unto the LORD, he arose from before the altar of the LORD, from kneeling on his knees with his hands spread up to heaven.

This verse is an example of someone in the Bible kneeling in prayer. The Hebrew word used here is *Kara*. It means kneel in reverence. Now reverence means to stand in awe of, be awed, to fear, honor, respect. Kneeling can be a sign that we are in awe of, fear, honor, **and respect God.**

Scripture: Mark 10:17, (KJV)

> And when he was gone forth into the way, there came one running, and kneeled to him, and asked him, Good Master, what shall I do that I may inherit eternal life?

This is another example of someone keeling. This is the story of the rich young ruler. The Greek word used here is *Gonupeteo*. It means the act of imploring aid, and of expressing reverence and honor. I believe that the rich young ruler was imploring aid, as he had a question for Jesus. Kneeling can be a sign of imploring aid, expressing reverence, and honor. To kneel in prayer can mean several things. We can kneel in awe of God. We can kneel to express our honor and respect. We can kneel before God to implore His aid.

Kneeling in prayer shows a humbleness of spirit. We humble ourselves before God. It helps us to remember that He is the one who is greater.

Scripture: Luke 22:41

> He withdrew about a stone's throw beyond them, knelt down and prayed, "Father, if you are willing, take this cup form me; yet not my will, but yours be done."

Other Scriptures:

Ezra 9:5

> Then, at the evening sacrifice, I rose from my self-abasement, with my tunic and cloak torn, and fell on my knees with my hands spread out to the Lord my God.

Acts 9:40

> Peter sent them all out of the room; then he got down on his knees and prayed. Turning toward the dead woman, he said, "Tabitha, get up." She opened her eyes, and seeing Peter she sat up.

Be very specific in what you are joining God to do. (Notice I said, "Joining God…")

Have a real conversation with Him. Tell Jesus how you feel about the way you look, your body size, your mind-set, how you feel inside and out, your doubts, eating habits, and your (fill in the blank). What is your mind-set? Have a conversation with Jesus.

Talk with Jesus about everything you have tried prior to this Bible study.

Take a few moments and sit in pure quietness. As God speaks…start writing.

Ask God to order your steps. Ask God for your ears to be opened, and your mind to be clear.

Week 1 ~ Day 1

Dear God,

Love ~
Date ~

Scripture: Psalm 37:23

The Lord makes firm the steps of the one who delights in him (NIV).

The Lord directs the steps of the godly. He delights in every detail of their lives (NLT).

Prayer: (You can pray this as a personal prayer by inserting "my" or "I" or you can pray for the community as printed below.)

This is the day the Lord has made, let us rejoice and be glad! Dear heavenly Father, take our (or you can pray my) hand, heart, and mind as we embark on this most beautiful journey of soul care, total life-altering, and complete, healthy journey with You. Lord, realign our thoughts, and help us to look at food, our habits, and our everyday life with fresh eyes. Not our will, Lord, but Thy will be done. Today, we take the first step to surrendering our will to Yours. Today, we step forward, ready to get to the root of it. In the amazing and all-powerful name of Jesus. ~Amen.

Prepare:

What do we need (you need) to fall on your knees to pray about? Removal of wounds? Release of weight? Removal of the pain of rejection? Removal of cravings? Removal or release of (you fill in the blank).

_____
_____
_____
_____
_____
_____
_____
_____
_____
_____
_____
_____
_____
_____
_____
_____

Make this day a day of great faith!

Day 2

Prayer position is bowing.

Reflection:

Write your thoughts in reference to Day 1 and the prayer position "kneeling."

_____
_____
_____
_____

The primary Hebrew word in the Old Testament translates worship to literally mean to bow down. The original Greek word in the New Testament has a similar meaning. Obviously, there is a close connection between worship and bowing down.

Whenever the Bible describes the activity in heaven we usually find worship at the center. And often the worship includes bowing down (Rev. 4:10; Rev. 5:14; Rev. 11:16). In fact, in Revelation nearly every time that the twenty-four elders are mentioned we find them bowing down before the throne. Other examples of bowing before God are found in Num. 20:6; Neh. 8:6; Matt. 2:11; and Luke 5:6-8.

To bow down before someone indicates two things. First it is a sign of honor and **respect**. It is recognition of the greatness of the one before whom you bow. Second, it is a sign of **submission**. By bowing before a king you are saying that he is greater than you are (you are the one bowing) and that your life is in his hands and under his power (you can't defend yourself with your face to the ground).

Why We Bow

In worship we declare God's greatness. He alone is worthy of glory, honor, and praise. One day all created beings will bow before Him and acknowledge that He is King of Kings and Lord of Lords (Phil. 2:9-10). In response to this truth we bow in surrender and adoration to our King. Our bowing may not always be physical (although it can be), but in our hearts we must bow before Him who is on the throne. Without this there is no true worship.

Prepare:

Write down your areas of struggle when it comes to your mind-set.

_____
_____
_____
_____
_____
_____
_____
_____
_____

Write your areas of strength.

_____
_____
_____
_____
_____
_____
_____
_____
_____

Scripture: Philippians 4:8

> Finally, brothers and sisters, whatever is true, whatever is noble, whatever is right, whatever is pure, whatever is lovely, whatever is admirable — if anything is excellent or praiseworthy — think about such things.

Prayer:

> Lord Jesus. Take my hand and lead me to a place of submission. God, I am ready to surrender. As I bow, receive all that I am laying at Your feet. Not my will, but Lord, may Your will be done in and through me. In the name of Jesus I pray. ~ Amen.

I pray that you soak in God's presence this week as we set this entire week aside for prayer and practicing each prayer position.

Day 3

This should be a Wednesday. Each Wednesday during our 49 days will be a day of fasting and praying. Please, if you have a medical condition, consult with your physician. If you must eat to take your prescribed medicine…do so.

Prayer position is prostrate.

Reflection:

Write your thoughts on the prayer position of bowing.

_____
_____
_____

Today we will focus on the "prostrate" prayer position plus spend the day fasting. Seek God's face and ask Him to give you strength to fast water, tea, and juice from 8:00 a.m. until 6:00 p.m. today.

Prostrate ~ lying stretched out on the ground with one's face downward

Deuteronomy 9:25

> I lay prostrate before the LORD those forty days and forty nights because the LORD had said he would destroy you.

Deuteronomy 9:20-30

> And the LORD was angry enough with Aaron to destroy him, but at that time I prayed for Aaron too. Also I took that sinful thing of yours, the calf you had made, and burned it in the fire. Then I crushed it and ground it to powder as fine as dust and threw the dust into a stream that flowed down the mountain. You also made the LORD angry at Taberah, at Massah and at Kibroth Hattaavah. And when the

Lord sent you out from Kadesh Barnea, he said, "Go up and take possession of the land I have given you." But you rebelled against the command of the Lord your God. You did not trust him or obey him. You have been rebellious against the Lord ever since I have known you. I lay prostrate before the Lord those forty days and forty nights because the Lord had said he would destroy you. I prayed to the Lord and said, "Sovereign Lord, do not destroy your people, your own inheritance that you redeemed by your great power and brought out of Egypt with a mighty hand. Remember your servants Abraham, Isaac and Jacob. Overlook the stubbornness of this people, their wickedness and their sin. Otherwise, the country from which you brought us will say, 'Because the Lord was not able to take them into the land he had promised them, and because he hated them, he brought them out to put them to death in the wilderness.' But they are your people, your inheritance that you brought out by your great power and your outstretched arm."

Ezra 10:1 (The People's Confession of Sin)

While Ezra was praying and confessing, weeping and throwing himself down before the house of God, a large crowd of Israelites—men, women and children—gathered around him. They too wept bitterly.

Joshua 7:6, Matthew 26:39 (Jesus in Gethsemane), and Mark 14:35

Study throughout the day: Isaiah 58 (break up the chapter with reading verses 1-3 in the morning, 4-6 in the afternoon, and 7-14 in the evening).

Prayer:

Lord, allow me to hear You. In the name of Jesus I pray. ~ Amen

Find time today to lay out on the floor with your face downward and pray in silence. (No music, television, etc.) Lie there praying, then be quiet until you hear God speak. I am bold enough to say, "You will hear Him." I truly believe you will.

Day 3

Write what God is speaking to you today. I believe God is going to speak clearly to each of you.

Just Doodle

Day 4

Prayer position is walking.

Reflection:

Praying in different prayer positions each day has….

_____
_____
_____

Ready to take back territory? We are going to walk and pray.

Yes…adding in some exercise today just to get our mind cleared. Exercising is good for your mind, body, and spirit. I personally attend a deep-stretching class once per week. It relieves the stress I have put on my shoulders from a week's work. We have a choice. We can choose to exercise or not. However, I believe God allows us to move about to shake some things loose. Shaking the stress, the frustration, and the feelings of rejections away from attaching to our bodies that could eventually cause disease and illness.

2 Kings 4:35 (taking back territory)

Scripture: 2 Kings 4:30-35

But the child's mother said, "As surely as the LORD lives and as you live, I will not leave you." So he got up and followed her. Gehazi went on ahead and laid the staff on the boy's face, but there was no sound or response. So Gehazi went back to meet Elisha and told him, "The boy has not awakened." When Elisha reached the house, there was the boy lying dead on his couch. He went in, shut the door on the two of them and prayed to the LORD. Then he got on the bed and lay on the boy, mouth to mouth, eyes to eyes, hands to hands. As he stretched himself out on him, the boy's body grew warm. Elisha turned away and walked back and forth in the room and then got on the bed and stretched out on him once more. The boy sneezed seven times and opened his eyes.

In this Scripture the child's mother refused to give up.

The boy was dead.
Elisha went in, and shut the door, and together they prayed.
He stretched himself out on the boy.
The boy's body grew warm.
Elisha walked back and forth.
Stretched out on him ONCE more.
The boy sneezed seven times and opened his eyes.

Allow me to work backwards.

Seven times: 7 is the number of completion (the Bible study is 7 weeks). It's time to open your eyes and see all the Lord has for you. Just for you!

Elisha walked: walking back and forth…taking back territory!

Body grew warm: Holy Spirit, come! God says, you will have life and have it in abundance!

Stretched out: Yesterday we lay prostrate. We surrendered. Today we walk and take back territory!

Shut the door and prayed: Go to your secret place and pray.

Boy was dead: "Therefore, if anyone is in Christ, the new creation has come: The old has gone, the new is here!" (2 Corinthians 5:17).

It is time to take back territory. Make a list of what you desire to take back and begin to walk and pray.

_____ _____ _____
_____ _____ _____
_____ _____ _____
_____ _____ _____
_____ _____ _____

Walk and Pray

Around your home, in your neighborhood, in your place of work, at the park, around the mall, wherever you decide to walk, do so by taking back territory. When you are walking to take back territory, you can be in a place of spiritual warfare. I would suggest you pray a covering upon you for protection. The enemy is mad because you have made a commitment to live your life whole and surrendered to Jesus. As you walk and pray, this can be done with another person or with several people. Walk and pray.

Day 4

As you pray be sure you cover every area in prayer. Go the extra mile and begin to anoint areas (and you) as your walk and pray. Pray a prayer of protection upon you. Simply pray, "I claim protection over myself this day."

Scripture: 2 Chronicles 6:19-21

> Yet, Lord my God, give attention to your servant's prayer and his plea for mercy. Hear the cry and the prayer that your servant is praying in your presence. May your eyes be open toward this temple day and night, this place of which you said you would put your Name there. May you hear the prayer your servant prays toward this place. Hear the supplications of your servant and of your people Israel when they pray toward this place. Hear from heaven, your dwelling place; and when you hear, forgive.

Prayer:

> God, hear our prayers as we walk and take back territory. Lord, may we walk in Your power and authority in the name of Jesus. Father, we declare and decree that we are Yours. No weapon formed against us shall prosper. That what the devil meant for evil we know You meant it for our good, therefore, we take back all that the enemy has taken. He must release everything that belongs to us right now, in the name of Jesus. In the name of Jesus, we take back our healthy bodies. In the name of Jesus, we take back our healthy minds. In the name of Jesus we take back our strength and our dignity. In the name of Jesus, we take back our relationships. In the name of Jesus, we take back our finances. In the name of Jesus, we take back our neighborhoods and larger communities. In the name of Jesus, we take back (fill in the blank). Thank You, Father, for hearing our prayers. We will be reminded to give You all the glory honor and praise. Amen!

Prayer Notes:

Day 5

Prayer position is standing.

1 Kings 8:54-56

> When Solomon had finished all these prayers and supplications to the LORD, he rose from before the altar of the LORD, where he had been kneeling with his hands spread out toward heaven. He stood and blessed the whole assembly of Israel in a loud voice, saying: "Praise be to the LORD, who has given rest to his people Israel just as he promised."

1 Kings 8:22

> Then Solomon stood before the altar of the LORD in front of the whole assembly of Israel, spread out his hands toward heaven…

1 Kings 8:38

> …and when a prayer or plea is made by anyone among your people Israel — being aware of the afflictions of their own hearts, and spreading out their hands toward this temple —

Mark 11:24-25

> Therefore, I tell you, whatever you ask for in prayer, believe that you have received it, and it will be yours. And when you stand praying, if you hold anything against any one, forgive him, so that your Father in heaven may forgive you your sins.

Luke 18:13

> "But the tax collector stood at a distance. He would not even look up to heaven, but beat his breast and said, 'God have mercy on me, a sinner.' "

Nehemiah 9:5

And the Levites—Jeshua, Kadmiel, Bani, Hashabneiah, Sherebiah, Hodiah, Shebaniah and Pethahiah—said: "Stand up and praise the Lord your God, who is from everlasting to everlasting."

1 Samuel 1:9 (Hannah stood up)

Once when they had finished eating and drinking in Shiloh, Hannah stood up. Now Eli the priest was sitting on his chair by the doorpost of the Lord's house.

Scripture: Philippians 4:6-8

Do not be anxious about anything, but in every situation, by prayer and petition, with thanksgiving, present your requests to God. And the peace of God, which transcends all understanding, will guard your hearts and your minds in Christ Jesus. Finally, brothers and sisters, whatever is true, whatever is noble, whatever is right, whatever is pure, whatever is lovely, whatever is admirable—if anything is excellent or praiseworthy—think about such things.

Prayer:

Lord, may Your anointing flow in all of Your children. May we have good health. May we seek and thirst after You in spirit and in truth. Lord, we are available to You. Our storage is empty, and we say, "Fill us up Lord." May the power of Your resurrection be true in our lives this day and forever. ~ Amen.

Day 6

Prayer position is sitting.

1 Chronicles 17:16-27

> Then King David went in and sat before the Lord, and he said:
>
> "Who am I, Lord God, and what is my family, that you have brought me this far? And as if this were not enough in your sight, my God, you have spoken about the future of the house of your servant. You, Lord God, have looked on me as though I were the most exalted of men.
>
> "What more can David say to you for honoring your servant? For you know your servant, Lord. For the sake of your servant and according to your will, you have done this great thing and made known all these great promises.
>
> "There is no one like you, Lord, and there is no God but you, as we have heard with our own ears. And who is like your people Israel—the one nation on earth whose God went out to redeem a people for himself, and to make a name for yourself, and to perform great and awesome wonders by driving out nations from before your people, whom you redeemed from Egypt? You made your people Israel your very own forever, and you, Lord, have become their God.
>
> "And now, Lord, let the promise you have made concerning your servant and his house be established forever. Do as you promised, so that it will be established and that your name will be great forever. Then people will say, 'The Lord Almighty, the God over Israel, is Israel's God!' And the house of your servant David will be established before you.
>
> "You, my God, have revealed to your servant that you will build a house for him. So your servant has found courage to pray to you. You, Lord, are God! You have promised these good things to your servant. Now you have been pleased to bless

the house of your servant, that it may continue forever in your sight; for you, Lord, have blessed it, and it will be blessed forever."

Prayer:

Lord, as I sit meditating upon Your Word and reflecting on the beauty of Your righteousness, I ask You to speak to me. God, there is none like You. I want to fully surrender my life into Your hands. Breathe on me Lord and use me for Your glory today and always. Amen.

Day 7

Prayer position is with hands lifted.

2 Chronicles 6:12-14

> Then Solomon stood before the altar of the Lord in front of the whole assembly of Israel and spread out his hands. Now he had made a bronze platform, five cubits long, five cubits wide and three cubits high, and had placed it in the center of the outer court. He stood on the platform and then knelt down before the whole assembly of Israel and spread out his hands toward heaven. He said: "Lord, God of Israel, there is no God like you in heaven or on earth—you who keep your covenant of love with your servants who continue wholeheartedly in your way.

Psalm 63:4

> I will praise you as long as I live, and in your name I will lift up my hands.

1 Timothy 2:8

> Therefore I want the men everywhere to pray, lifting up holy hands without anger or disputing.

IMPORTANT ~ Whatever position your body is in, God is still paying attention, and the leading of the Holy Spirit is more important than the position as you yield to Him. The openness of your heart is ultimately what counts.

Reflect on Week 1.

Week 2 ~ Day 8

"Then the LORD replied: "Write down the revelation and make it plain on tablets so that a herald may run with it" (Habakkuk 2:2). I read somewhere that "if you don't know where you are going, you will never get there." I believe one of the most important activities you will do on this journey is to write things down as God speaks. Journal what He says. Capture what He deposits into your spirit. Yes, journal. It's been told as a life lesson that to achieve a goal, you must first know what your goal is, and then you must write down your goals in order to achieve them. Acknowledging your goals will allow you to intentionally move a thought into action in order to improve your walk on any journey of your life.

Writing goals on paper allows you to be conscious of your progress. Post your written goals so you may see them regularly. Near a mirror. In your office. In the bathroom. Once a goal is written you can reflect on it on a regular basis, and it becomes easier to witness the manifestation. When you write down your goals, you will see how God is answering or redirecting you.

Writing in your journal becomes meaningful to you. Writing your goals will help you stay focused even after the 49 days. Start by envisioning your goals. Complete a faith portrait from your goals and what you have visualized. This helps you stay on track with your goals. Prayer and visualization are powerful.

Journals

Journals are a powerful means of reflecting, processing, and living through each day. They allow space for you to write your innermost thoughts, healing, wounds, reflections, pain, past, present, and future. Journaling allows you to move forward with passion and intention. Writing and reflecting on your journal gives you an opportunity to experience good health and being willing to deal with past situations and heal. It's a process. At times it may be painful. However, keep pushing through. Journaling allows for repressed memories and past life situations to come to the surface, and gives you the ability and God's strength to deal with them in a healthier state. Write a Scripture in your journal each day on each morning. At night write in your journal how the Scripture manifested in your life during the day.

Assignment:

Complete a faith portrait (example on next page). Use the blank page following to complete your faith portrait. You will need glue, images, markers, and crayons.

Scripture: Philippians 4:8

> Finally, brothers and sisters, whatever is true, whatever is noble, whatever is right, whatever is pure, whatever is lovely, whatever is admirable — if anything is excellent or praiseworthy — think about such things.

Prayer:

> God, I desire to hear You. I desire to write the vision, make it plain, and run with it. Lord, I want to see Your will manifested in my life. ~ Amen.

Week 2 ~ Day 8

Faith Portrait

Mark 11:24

"Therefore I tell you, whatever you ask for in prayer, believe that you have received it, and it will be yours." NIV

Faith Portrait

Use this space to glue images to design your Faith Portrait

Day 9

Reflection:

Write your vision. Make it plain. What will be your weakness? Strength (on this journey)?

Be very specific in what you are joining God to do. Remember we cannot do this in our own strength.

_____
_____
_____
_____
_____
_____
_____
_____
_____
_____
_____
_____
_____
_____
_____
_____
_____
_____
_____
_____

Ask God to order your steps throughout this journey. Ask God for your ears to be opened, and your mind to be clear.

Take a few moments and sit in pure quietness. As God speaks, list your wounds. List your past pain and rejections. Turn these things over to the Lord.

_____
_____
_____
_____
_____
_____
_____
_____
_____
_____
_____
_____
_____
_____
_____
_____
_____
_____
_____
_____
_____
_____
_____
_____
_____
_____
_____
_____

(Need more space? Write in your journal and take all the space you need to express your innermost pain.)

Scripture: Read Romans 12:1-2

Philippians 4:8

> Finally, brothers and sisters, whatever is true, whatever is noble, whatever is right, whatever is pure, whatever is lovely, whatever is admirable—if anything is excellent or praiseworthy—think about such things.

Prayer:

Lord, I need You. Please help me as I expose myself to You and pull back the bandage that has previously covered my wounds. I know You already know what I have been dealing with, but today I desire to be vulnerable and be transparent with You and trust the process on this journey of my healing. God, please give me Your strength to walk this out to completion.

Just Doodle

Day 10

Reflection:

Record your thoughts about the previous day.

Day 10 is the day to cleanse! It's about cleansing your mind.

We are going to cleanse our mind of all the past and present junk we have told ourselves about life, relationships, strengths, weaknesses, food, health, weight, age, etc. Today we shall declare that those messages we continue to play on our mental tape will cease. Time to stop playing those past negative messages over and over and over again. You are only repeating a dialogue that is unhealthy for you. When you do so you are continuing to open the wounds that you are working to heal.

From a small sampling of my coaching clients, more than 80 percent of women I spoke with experience self-deprecating thoughts about their total being. This included their weight, personal and professional life, and the opinions of what they believe others have of them. What happens is that we find ourselves in a state of replaying these thoughts regularly and that's unhealthy. It's time to turn those deadly thoughts into speaking life over yourself. The Bible says in Proverbs 18:20-21, "From the fruit of their mouth a person's stomach is filled; with the harvest of their lips they are satisfied. The tongue has the power of life and death, and those who love it will eat its fruit."

It's time to stop repeating and reliving your fears, past events, past messages, pain, and rejection. Stop living in your insecurities.

Write down things you believe you need to cleanse from your mind. If you need extra space, write in your journal. Be as open and honest to yourself and God as possible. If you recognize triggers, write those down and write "triggers" beside those words.

_____
_____
_____
_____
_____
_____
_____
_____
_____
_____
_____
_____
_____
_____
_____

Day 10

Think about a body cleanse/detox. It is designed to remove artificial flavors and chemical substances from your diet. This helps prepare your body to live a healthier and more natural lifestyle.

We are going to do the same for Day 10, but with cleansing/detoxing our thoughts. As you pray throughout Day 10, trust that God is going to remove any and all negativity and lies that have clouded your mind. This cleanse is going to give you clarity of mind. The fog is going to dissipate. Trust God.

In doing a body cleanse/detox there are steps to take. Usually you wake and drink green tea or warm lemon water. After a few hours you drink some sort of green smoothie along with taking a multivitamin and possibly a probiotic. For lunch you have another smoothie, and maybe take some sort of omega supplement. If you're lucky you may have a midafternoon smoothie, then of course one at dinner. It throws your body into shock to lose. **BUT** the key to a body cleanse/detox is to drink plenty of water. Think about a body cleanse/detox you have participated in previously. What steps did you take?

Day 10 (a Wednesday) is also a day of fasting. For the cleanse we are going to drink plenty of LIVING WATER! As you are led, please pray and read Scripture throughout the day. The water is for flushing purposes. It's getting rid of things that do not belong…mind, body, and spirit. The water is also for living purposes to give you strength to live your life worthy of the call of Christ.

Drink half your body weight in water. Take your body weight and divide by two. Drink this plus 10 more ounces. Consider this your tithe and offering in water.

As it relates to physical foods…eat as God leads you to eat and realize that not everyone is able to go for a complete fast. Seek God and ask Him how you should participate. Please…if you have to take food with medication, eat.

Day 10 ~ Pray and give permission for God to alter your mind-set.

What is God calling you to do? Ask. Listen. Journal.

Scripture: Romans 12:1-2

Therefore, I urge you, brothers and sisters, in view of God's mercy, to offer your bodies as a living sacrifice, holy and pleasing to God—this is your true and proper worship. Do not conform to the pattern of this world, but be transformed by the renewing of your mind. Then you will be able to test and approve what God's will is—his good, pleasing and perfect will.

Philippians 4:8

Finally, brothers and sisters, whatever is true, whatever is noble, whatever is right, whatever is pure, whatever is lovely, whatever is admirable—if anything is excellent or praiseworthy—think about such things.

Prepare:

Write down your areas of struggle.

Write your areas of strength.

Prayer:

Lord, help us deal with our mind-set. We desire to purge all that is not of You. Thank You for allowing us to start with offering our bodies as a living sacrifice, holy and pleasing to You. Lord, help us to be transformed by the renewing of our minds. We desire to test and approve what Your will is…not our will, and we desire for our will to be good, pleasing, and perfect in alignment with Your will. God, we give You permission to "check us" each time we think of things that are not true. Expose the lies and shine light on the truth. As we eat…help us to do a self-evaluation. As we have thoughts…help us to process so we can get to the root of it. As we look at our bodies…help us to see the beauty You created us to be. God, we give You permission to check our hearts. We desire our minds to be cleansed of anything that is not of You or does not line up with your will for our lives. We desire to drink from the living water of truth, light, and life. ~ Amen.

May this day be the best day yet!

Scriptures to soak in to allow the detox to continue:

1 Peter 3:10
Colossians 4:6
Ephesians 4:29
Proverbs 15:4
Matthew 15:11
Proverbs 21:23
Proverbs 31:26
Psalm 34:13
Psalm 141:3
Proverbs 12:18-19

Just Doodle

Day 11

Reflection:

Write your experience from the day of cleansing. How did it go for you?

Once we allow God to reveal things to us, He begins to expose areas of our lives we have tried to hide. Sometimes that is difficult to handle. I would encourage you to go with the flow of the Holy Spirit.

Find time today to bask in the Lord's presence. Google defines bask as to: lie exposed to warmth and light, typically from the sun, for relaxation and pleasure. Google defines soak as to: make or allow (something) to become thoroughly wet by immersing it in liquid.

Bask – Expose yourself to God's presence.

Soak – Allow yourself to be immersed in God's presence.

Getting to the Root of It: A Healing Balm of Freedom is about holistic health. Let's be honest. We have tried to be free by drinking to numb the pain, but when we return to reality our life is staring at us in our face. We have tried to suffocate our pain by sleeping the day away only to wake with the same condition. We have tried to replace a bad relationship with a new one to only find we are attracted to the same type of person. We have tried to drop the weight on our own with pills, not eating, abstaining from certain foods, surgery, or crazy exercise. We wonder why we accomplish a goal to return to business as usual soon thereafter. God has shown me it is about our relationship with Him. Our mind-set has everything to do with each area we will focus on during this Bible study.

> *Getting to the Root of It: A Healing Balm of Freedom* is about availing yourself to prayer, and listening to God's directions. He is telling us what to do, when to do it, and how to do it.

How often have you tried to gain a new skill, live life differently, and/or diet because you saw pictures or know someone who was successful on a particular program? God's Word says, "We are uniquely made." A diet that may work for one may not work for you or me. *Getting to the Root of It: A Healing Balm of Freedom* is about availing yourself to prayer, and listening to God's directions. He is telling us what to do, when to do it, and how to do it.

Day 11

Prepare:

When you read Psalm 139:14-17, what is God speaking to you?

_____
_____
_____
_____
_____
_____
_____
_____

In reading Psalm 139:14-17, where do you wrestle?

_____
_____
_____
_____
_____
_____
_____
_____
_____

Scripture: Psalm 139:13-17

> For you created my inmost being; you knit me together in my mother's womb. I praise you because I am fearfully and wonderfully made; your works are wonderful, I know that full well. My frame was not hidden from you when I was made in the secret place, when I was woven together in the depths of the earth. Your eyes saw my unformed body; all the days ordained for me were written in your book before one of them came to be. How precious to me are your thoughts, God! How vast is the sum of them!

Philippians 4:8

> Finally, brothers and sisters, whatever is true, whatever is noble, whatever is right, whatever is pure, whatever is lovely, whatever is admirable—if anything is excellent or praiseworthy—think about such things.

Prayer:

> Lord, may we rest in Your glory as we walk this journey each day. ~ Amen.

What is God speaking right now?

Day 12 – 14

Reflection:

How do you see yourself on this journey?

_____
_____
_____
_____
_____

Continue to spend time in prayer and seeking what God has for you by meditating on these Scriptures:

<u>Faith</u> ~ Galatians 2:20: I have been crucified with Christ and I no longer live, but Christ lives in me. The life I now live in the body, I live by faith in the Son of God, who loved me and gave himself for me.

_____
_____
_____
_____
_____
_____

<u>Surrender</u> ~ Mark 8:35: For whoever wants to save their life will lose it, but whoever loses their life for me and for the gospel will save it.

_____
_____
_____
_____
_____

Know Him ~ Philippians 3:10 (KJV): That I may know him, and the power of his resurrection, and the fellowship of his sufferings, being made conformable unto his death.

_____
_____
_____
_____
_____
_____
_____

Prepare:

Write down your areas of struggle.

_____
_____
_____
_____
_____
_____
_____
_____

Write your areas of strength.

_____
_____
_____
_____
_____
_____
_____
_____

Scripture: Philippians 4:8

> Finally, brothers and sisters, whatever is true, whatever is noble, whatever is right, whatever is pure, whatever is lovely, whatever is admirable—if anything is excellent or praiseworthy—think about such things.

Prayer:

> Jesus, we want to know You and the power of Your resurrection. ~ Amen.

Week 3 ~ Day 15

Reflection:

Thoughts of Faith, Surrender, and Know Him.

_____
_____
_____
_____
_____
_____
_____
_____
_____
_____
_____

The most difficult part of a journey is waiting. There are times when we may confuse our destination with our journey. Through this process we must stay in communion with Jesus and resist trying to control the process.

The process can be the most fruitful. Living an abundant life is our walk with God. Please do not miss out on the journey of following each day's content and prompter. Enjoy the richness of your prayer conversation with God as He leads you to releasing the weight, stress, worry, concern, burden, etc., that life has thrown your way. Please do not miss out on the journey of growing a more intimate relationship with Jesus by rushing towards the destination.

Take this journey for what is it. Do not try to create something that it is not. Do not try to manufacture a destination. The only way you can get to your destination is to talk with God each day and do as He instructs you. "Obedience is better than sacrifice" (1 Samuel 15:22).

Don't focus on the results or the outcome. Stay present and enjoy the journey. Get to know "you" differently based upon listening to God each day and being obedient to everything He is calling you to do.

Do not become frustrated. Our frustration comes from focusing on the wrong things… such as focusing on the destination when we have 34 days to go. Focus on the journey, including the struggle on the way to the destination. There is value in the journey, which oftentimes becomes the struggle as you go through it. Key word: through.

Romans 7:14-25

> We know that the law is spiritual; but I am unspiritual, sold as a slave to sin. I do not understand what I do. For what I want to do I do not do, but what I hate I do. And if I do what I do not want to do, I agree that the law is good. As it is, it is no longer I myself who do it, but it is sin living in me. For I know that good itself does not dwell in me, that is, in my sinful nature. For I have the desire to do what is good, but I cannot carry it out. For I do not do the good I want to do, but the evil I do not want to do—this I keep on doing. Now if I do what I do not want to do, it is no longer I who do it, but it is sin living in me that does it. So I find this law at work: Although I want to do good, evil is right there with me. For in my inner being I delight in God's law; but I see another law at work in me, waging war against the law of my mind and making me a prisoner of the law of sin at work within me. What a wretched man I am! Who will rescue me from this body that is subject to death? Thanks be to God, who delivers me through Jesus Christ our Lord!

The struggle is real. The battle is before you, but alignment with God and His Word is most important.

Are you in alignment with God? Explain:

_____
_____
_____
_____
_____
_____
_____
_____
_____
_____

How do we win the battle? How do we bring ourselves—body, soul, and spirit—into alignment with God?

1) We have to study and know God's Word. It is the greatest weapon. This is living water.

2) We have to get in right alignment with the Word of God. Knowing God's Word is not enough.

3) When we know God's Word we know that we must take our fleshly thoughts captive (2 Cor. 10:3-5).

4) We have to dwell with the Lord in and out of season. We are all ministers of the Gospel. Therefore, we are to be "prepared in season and out of season; correct, rebuke and encourage—with great patience and careful instruction" (2 Tim. 4:2).

The more time we spend with Jesus, the more strength we have to continue the journey and "Pray to Lose." The more time we spend with Jesus, the more secure we will become. The more we are intentional with aligning with God's Word, the more we will flow under His anointing.

What will you do to stay in alignment with God's Word?

_____
_____
_____
_____

Prepare:

Write down your areas of struggle.

_____
_____
_____
_____
_____
_____
_____
_____
_____
_____

Write your areas of strength.

_____
_____
_____
_____
_____
_____
_____
_____
_____
_____

Scripture: Romans 5:3-5 (NLT)

We can rejoice, too, when we run into problems and trials, for we know that they help us develop endurance. And endurance develops strength of character, and character strengthens our confident hope of salvation. And this hope will not lead to disappointment. For we know how dearly God loves us, because he has given us the Holy Spirit to fill our hearts with his love.

Prayer:

Lord, help me stay focused on You. I want to know You and the power of Your resurrection.

Days 16 and 17

(This is Day 16 and 17. For day 17 which is Wednesday remember to fast and pray.)

Reflection: Share thoughts about the previous day.

___

Are you in alignment with God's Word? Explain.

___

We will look at the importance of living without the load.

Why are we carrying this load (whatever you identify as a load)? It is time to lay this (stress, weight, worry, relationships, finances, mind-set, etc.) aside. The more we try to handle this on our own, the deeper we find ourselves taking on the things God has not called us to do. "These" things…this load…becomes a distraction.

2 Kings 4:1-7

> The wife of a man from the company of the prophets cried out to Elisha, "Your servant my husband is dead, and you know that he revered the Lord. But now his creditor is coming to take my two boys as his slaves." Elisha replied to her, "How can I help you? Tell me, what do you have in your house?" "Your servant has nothing there at all," she said, "except a small jar of olive oil." Elisha said, "Go around and ask all your neighbors for empty jars. Don't ask for just a few. Then go inside and shut the door behind you and your sons. Pour oil into all the jars, and as each is filled, put it to one side." She left him and shut the door behind her and her sons. They brought the jars to her and she kept pouring. When all the jars were full, she said to her son, "Bring me another one." But he replied, "There is not a jar left." Then the oil stopped flowing. She went and told the man of God, and he said, "Go, sell the oil and pay your debts. You and your sons can live on what is left."

The woman in 2 Kings 4:1-7 solicited help from Elisha in her time of crisis. He asked her, "How can I help you? Tell me, what do you have in your house?" Notice her reply. She says, "Your servant has nothing at all." Then she adds, "except a little oil."

Two things I would like to point out.

1) Notice that she first said, "I have nothing at all." Was that really true? How often do we say that we have nothing? Why is it that we don't look at what we have no matter how big or how small?

2) Notice she adds, "Except a little oil."

When it comes to our journey we have to ask the question, "What do I have in my house?" "What do I have in my temple?"

If you haven't noticed already, God is connecting our health/weight with our thoughts/mind-set, our overall life, and living.

Three steps to process.

1) Be obedient to the instructions. Read 2 Kings 4:1-7. Notice she was obedient to the instructions. It is important to follow God throughout these 49 days. You may have many questions, but please do not abort the process. Follow His instructions. What do you need to be obedient?

   _____
   _____
   _____
   _____
   _____
   _____
   _____
   _____

2) Block the distractions. Again, when you read 2 Kings 4:1-7 you will notice they shut the door behind them and started filling the jars. What doors do you have to shut so you can continue the journey? What do you have to let go of? What is God speaking?

   _____
   _____
   _____
   _____
   _____
   _____
   _____

3) Enjoy the benefits of the overflow. Again, when you read 2 Kings 4:1-7 you will notice her "except a little oil" filled jar after jar. It wasn't until the last jar was filled the oil ceased. Additionally, once she went to Elisha she had enough to pay off her creditors and live off the rest (the overflow). What's your overflow? How are you going to live in your overflow after you have decided to live without the load?

   _____
   _____
   _____
   _____
   _____
   _____
   _____

Philippians 4:8

> Finally, brothers and sisters, whatever is true, whatever is noble, whatever is right, whatever is pure, whatever is lovely, whatever is admirable—if anything is excellent or praiseworthy—think about such things.

Prepare:

Write down your areas of struggle.

_____
_____
_____
_____
_____
_____

Write your areas of strength.

_____
_____
_____
_____
_____
_____

Scripture: Romans 5:3-5 (NLT)

> We can rejoice, too, when we run into problems and trials, for we know that they help us develop endurance. And endurance develops strength of character, and character strengthens our confident hope of salvation. And this hope will not lead to disappointment. For we know how dearly God loves us, because he has given us the Holy Spirit to fill our hearts with his love.

Prayer:

_____
_____
_____
_____
_____
_____
_____

Day 18

Reflection:

Review the prayer positions from Week 1. Identify those positions that were comfortable and those that were not so comfortable.

_____
_____
_____
_____
_____
_____
_____

How are you feeling? Do you sense clarity of mind, body, and spirit?

_____
_____
_____
_____
_____
_____
_____

How often do we look in the mirror and focus on our flaws? I am amazed of the times I can look in the mirror and one day my eyebrows are perfect and the very next day I see where my brows need immediate cleanup. One day they are fine. Overnight they need plucking and shaped. In a similar way we may find that some plucking needs to take place in our lives—such as toxic relationships or bad habits. It all starts with prayer. I know when I take a trip to the salon to have my eyebrows arched there are times I must pray first, considering the pain that will follow.

Prayer is necessary to make transition less painful.

Let's use Philippians 4:6-7 as our step-by-step instructions in helping us transition by plucking out bad habits from our lives.

Step One: Do not be anxious about anything.

Step Two: But in everything, by prayer and petition, with thanksgiving, present your requests to God.

Step Three: And the peace of God, which transcends all understanding, will guard your hearts and minds in Christ Jesus.

Yes! The Bible…God's Word already has the answers for us to follow.

When we pray first about the thing(s) we need to change in our lives, God's peace will act as a supernatural numbing solution. When the numbness wears off we will remember what happened, but we are better able to deal with it.

Is there anything you need to pluck out of your life to regain your health holistically? Explain.

_____
_____
_____
_____
_____
_____
_____
_____

Scripture: Psalm 139:13-17

> For you created my inmost being; you knit me together in my mother's womb. I praise you because I am fearfully and wonderfully made; your works are wonderful, I know that full well. My frame was not hidden from you when I was made in the secret place, when I was woven together in the depths of the earth. Your eyes saw my unformed body; all the days ordained for me were written in your book before one of them came to be. How precious to me are your thoughts, God! How vast is the sum of them!

Prayer:

> Lord, thank You for making me fearfully and wonderfully. I have decided to embrace me. ~ Amen.

Days 19 – 21

(This should be your Friday through Sunday if you had a Monday start of the 49 days)

Reflection:

What's working for you? Where do you struggle?
_____
_____
_____
_____
_____
_____
_____
_____
_____
_____
_____
_____
_____
_____
_____
_____

Weekend exercise. It's challenging, but it is necessary.

If possible use a poster board to complete the following.

Make two columns.

Column 1: Write down every food and drink that you consume over the weekend (Friday, Saturday, Sunday). Don't forget items such as butter, sour cream, extra cheese, potato chips, coffeehouse, etc.

Column 2: Write down every person in your circle of influence (positive or negative). Draw a line under the last person you write down whom you consider your circle of influence. After that last name (the one you drew a line under)…write down individuals whom you have been in conflict with over the last two (2) **YEARS**.

Draw a line from the person who is listed in Column 2 to a food in Column 1.

Now ask yourself this question and write the answer in your journal. What is your relationship to the foods and drinks you consume on certain days when you are in certain moods?

Scripture: Your Scripture choice.

Philippians 4:8

> Finally, brothers and sisters, whatever is true, whatever is noble, whatever is right, whatever is pure, whatever is lovely, whatever is admirable—if anything is excellent or praiseworthy—think about such things.

Prepare:

What do you need to put in place to hear from God and be obedient to His instructions as you lay aside the weight?

_____
_____
_____
_____
_____
_____
_____
_____
_____
_____
_____
_____
_____

Prayer:

> Lord, help me understand the relationship I have with food and the people who bring me joy, and those who create internal conflict for me. Lord, help me to focus on the love You have for me and help me stay present with You at all times. In the name of Jesus I pray. ~ Amen.

Week 4 ~ Day 22

Reflection:

Share thoughts about the previous day.

_____
_____
_____
_____
_____
_____
_____
_____
_____
_____

Welcome to Day 22.

Today we are going to deal with dying to self!

The 3 Cs:

Critical Spirit
Comparing Spirit
Controlling Spirit

Trust me. Our joy can be destroyed with a critical spirit. A critical spirit will alter our attitude. A critical spirit can alter our emotions. If we are emotional eaters…we eat the wrong things, which starts the yo-yo dieting…this can lead to weight gain. The cycle starts all over again.

A critical spirit is an obsessive attitude of criticism and faultfinding. A person with a critical spirit is obsessed with complaining. This is different from constructive criticism. When we are critical it throws off triggers in our bodies. This could possibly send a signal to eat to give us comfort.

Likewise, a comparing spirit is a thief of joy. Our joy is actually robbed when we compare ourselves to someone else. Our joy is then being suffocated by playing the comparison game. When we play the comparison game we end up both joyless and hopeless. No matter how often you compare yourself with others, you will always come up short (positive or negative). When we do it as a "positive" we are then puffing ourselves up with pride and that becomes a sin. A comparing spirit is obsessed with self. The cycle starts all over again. If we have lost our joy we then think, "Who cares?" and with this attitude we may easily fall into eating just because of needing something that brings us comfort.

This leads us to a controlling spirit. When someone has a controlling spirit, the person desperately tries to dictate how everything is to be done. This spirit is motivated by fear that something will not get done "if I don't do it" or something will go wrong "if I don't do it" and that fear drives one to "manipulate" situations with hopes it will go the way the person desires. Oh…by the way…manipulation is a spirit of witchcraft. Yep…you got it; the cycle starts all over again. If I can't control, I might as well eat.

> We are four full weeks into our *Getting to the Root of It* commitment and some of us have already thrown in the towel. What's easier? Living in the land of wounds, pain, and rejection? OR…praying and being obedient to God's directions, and get to the root of it?

What is this cycle? Walking in unfamiliar territory. Being uncomfortable with something new and too afraid to get uncomfortable…so we eat emotionally, we walk around hopeless with the sense of feeling insignificant, and we start trying to control things or even move to manipulate. This is a heavy weight that is placed upon our shoulders that we cannot handle, and we lose sleep, have restless nights, eat whatever is before us, worry, stack our thinking with negatives, and everything is seen as a doom-and-gloom life expectancy.

Let's agree. It's time to die to self.

We are four full weeks into our *Getting to the Root of It* commitment and some of us have already thrown in the towel. What's easier? Living in the land of wounds, pain, and rejection? Living with what's familiar? Going on crazy diets and exercising 24/7 to have temporary results? (87 percent of individuals who lose weight in this way gain the weight back, plus. ~ American Medical Journal, May 2015.) OR…praying and being obedient to God's directions, and get to the root of it?

For most people we would say praying, obedience, and getting to the root, and yet we still struggle.

We must remind ourselves that our lives are about dying as well as rising. There is no resurrection without death. It is time to die to self!

Question:

How can you bless the dying and the rising of your life, knowing that both are in the name of the Lord?

_____
_____
_____
_____
_____
_____
_____
_____
_____
_____

Scripture:

Today let's ask God to give us a Scripture to meditate on these remaining days.

Philippians 4:8

> Finally, brothers and sisters, whatever is true, whatever is noble, whatever is right, whatever is pure, whatever is lovely, whatever is admirable—if anything is excellent or praiseworthy—think about such things.

Prepare:

Write down your areas of struggle.

_____
_____
_____
_____
_____
_____
_____
_____

Write your areas of strength.

Write a personal prayer:

Prayer:

Father God, we bless You. We want to do Your will. We freely place our whole being in your hands. ~ Amen.

I am praying for all of us. I discern things are uphill from here, but we must be obedient.

Day 23

Reflection:

What's going well? What areas are you struggling with?

___
___
___
___
___

From one of my audible experiences with Jesus: He asked me two questions that actually made me stop in my tracks and cry. Here are the questions: 1) "Why not listen to Me and live?" and 2) "What is the resistance to 'praying and living life' here on earth as your best self?" My reply: "Why is this difficult at times?"

Think back to Day 22. It is about dying to self continuously.

Prayer suggestions

1) **Pray with excitement, expecting God to answer.**

   Pray by thanking God for life, breath, if you have movement of limbs, blood flowing, heart pumping, vision, etc.

2) **Pray God-centered prayers.**

   Do not focus on you. Focus on God. Come to God with your heart yet come away from that time of prayer with His heart.

3) **Pray with persistence.**

   Be persistent in your prayers—ask, seek, knock. Keep praying. Do not throw in the towel.

4) Pray believing God will answer, and say, "Thank You" when He answers.

<u>Exercise:</u> Take a jar. It can be a mason jar. Bedazzle it and call it your "jar of prayers." Have 3x5 index cards sitting next to the jar. Write down a prayer request with the date. Place the card inside the jar. At the end of every week go through the jar and see just how many prayers were answered. Prayers that were not answered that week should be placed back in the jar until the following week. The cards with prayers that were answered should be taped inside your journal under a heading "Answered Prayers." Watch God fill your journal with answered prayers.

Did you know that praying patients who entered open-heart surgery were three times more likely to survive the surgery than people with no spiritual background? Yes. That's true. (*Reader's Digest*, 2007).

We are the patients seeking a healthy lifestyle with the benefit of dropping pounds, inches, negative thoughts, stress, worry, etc. Write why you are on this journey of Getting to the Root of It.

_____
_____
_____
_____
_____
_____
_____
_____
_____
_____
_____
_____
_____
_____

Scripture: The one you have chosen to continue our remaining days on this journey.

Matthew 7:7-8

> "Ask and it will be given to you; seek and you will find; knock and the door will be opened to you. For everyone who asks receives; he who seeks finds; and to him who knocks, the door will be opened."

Philippians 4:6-8

> Do not be anxious about anything, but in every situation, by prayer and petition, with thanksgiving, present your requests to God. And the peace of God, which transcends all understanding, will guard your hearts and your minds in Christ

Jesus. Finally, brothers and sisters, whatever is true, whatever is noble, whatever is right, whatever is pure, whatever is lovely, whatever is admirable—if anything is excellent or praiseworthy—think about such things.

Scripture: Philippians 4:8

Finally, brothers and sisters, whatever is true, whatever is noble, whatever is right, whatever is pure, whatever is lovely, whatever is admirable—if anything is excellent or praiseworthy—think about such things.

Prepare:

How will you prepare to continue this journey after you have reached Day 49?

How will you adjust your mind-set?

Prayer:

Father, I thank You for being my heavenly Father. I am grateful You are always walking with me and speaking into my life. I love You with all of my heart. Give me the faith and joy to communion with You daily. Help me to trust in You more. I give my burdens and anxieties to You. Please help me (share specific concerns). Thank You for hearing and answering this prayer. Every good and perfect gift is from You. Thank You for giving me what's best. In the name of Jesus I pray. ~ Amen.

Just Doodle

Day 24

Reflection:

What's going well? What areas are you struggling in?

_____
_____
_____
_____
_____
_____
_____
_____
_____
_____
_____
_____
_____
_____
_____

Do what you love!

Never lower your expectations. Don't do it! The exact moment you lower your expectations things begin to shift. After a while you will begin to resist not going after what you love to do because of fear, anxiety, insecurities, low self-esteem, etc.

Transparent Moment:

During one of the most difficult times of my life I started experiencing anxiety whenever I would stand to preach God's Word. I had prepared. I had studied. I had written the sermons to proclaim the Gospel of Jesus. Yes, I would stand and feel as if the enemy were choking the life out of me. My mouth would become dry, and I would at times feel like fainting.

For a year I would not accept invitations to preach. I started telling myself that people really did not want to hear me. I told myself that I was not qualified. I lowered my expectations of me, and of God. However, I knew God called me to preach and to teach. I knew God called me to a ministry of prayer.

Many of us on this journey have lowered our expectations with our holistic health. We have decided that we will always be this body size, think the way we think, act the way we act, etc. STOP! The devil is a liar. You are better than that! We are better than that!

I had to deal with the root cause. You will have to deal with the root cause of whatever you have decided to forgo and back away from although God has called you to it.

What do you love to do? Why do you love to do it? Are you doing it?

_____
_____
_____
_____
_____
_____
_____
_____
_____

Is it running? But weight is holding you back? Start somewhere. Begin with leisure walking. Then start walking faster every few sections on the sidewalk. Return to a normal walk. After a few minutes, walk faster, then start a jog for three seconds, then return to walking your normal pace. After a while you will increase that time. Please note: Always talk with your physician before beginning any physical exercising beyond walking.

Make a list.

Take a few risks.

Identify one thing and become an expert in that area.

Our weight (body and life) has everything to do with every fabric of our being. Trust God. Trust the process. Keep journaling, and watch God move in more amazing ways in your life.

Scripture: The Scripture you are using, plus…

Philippians 4:13 (NKJV)

> I can do all things through Christ who strengthens me.

Philippians 4:6-9 (NKJV):

Be anxious for nothing, but in everything by prayer and supplication, with thanksgiving, let your requests be made known to God; and the peace of God, which surpasses all understanding, will guard your hearts and minds through Christ Jesus. Finally, brethren, whatever things are true, whatever things are noble, whatever things are just, whatever things are pure, whatever things are lovely, whatever things are of good report, if there is any virtue and if there is anything praiseworthy—meditate on these things. The things which you learned and received and heard and saw in me, these do, and the God of peace will be with you.

Scripture: Philippians 4:8

Finally, brothers and sisters, whatever is true, whatever is noble, whatever is right, whatever is pure, whatever is lovely, whatever is admirable—if anything is excellent or praiseworthy—think about such things.

Prepare:

What will you begin working on that you have been avoiding?

_____
_____
_____
_____
_____
_____
_____
_____
_____
_____
_____

What will it take for you to stay the course?

_____
_____
_____
_____
_____
_____
_____
_____
_____

Prayer:

God, I desire to return to my first love—You! Please show me the way to live the life You have called me to live. Lord, forgive me for departing from the path You have set for me out of fear, insecurity, and low self-esteem. God, grant me a measure of Your grace, wisdom, and power. Lord, today I will walk boldly in all You have for me with confidence. Thank You in advance for the amazing favor that will fall upon me. In the name of Jesus I pray. ~ Amen.

Day 25

Reflection:

Write your thoughts from the poster board exercise.

_____
_____
_____
_____
_____
_____
_____
_____

Dealing with Negative Thoughts:

Whenever you have a negative thought…write it down. We are not doing this exercise for guilt or shame; we are doing it to see just how many negative thoughts we have within a day.

Transparent Moment:

As I completed this exercise early on my journey I was surprised by how many thoughts I had in one day that did not line up with God's Word. I put those thoughts in my prayer jar (remember the prayer jar exercise) and started praying over the thoughts I had that did not line up with the Lord. God has been answering my prayers. I have noticed the weight that has been lifted from my shoulders as my mind-set has changed from negative thoughts to thoughts of God's will and instructions for my life. If I do not follow through with the negative thoughts, I have noticed they are decreasing, and I'm replacing them with prayer and God's Word. "Therefore, there is now no condemnation for those who are in Christ Jesus…" (Romans 8:1).

Today, let's fast from negative thoughts.

Prepare:

Write down your areas of struggle.

_____
_____
_____
_____
_____
_____
_____
_____

Write your areas of strength.

_____
_____
_____
_____
_____
_____
_____
_____
_____

Scripture: Philippians 4:8

Finally, brothers and sisters, whatever is true, whatever is noble, whatever is right, whatever is pure, whatever is lovely, whatever is admirable—if anything is excellent or praiseworthy—think about such things.

Prayer:

God, renew my thinking today. Help me to see my thoughts and then turn them over to You. Lord, touch my mind today. Give me a peace and a comfort as I process my thoughts. Lord, may I look at my poster board and see where I may be struggling with emotional eating. God, I simply turn everything over to You. It's more than weight…it's my lifestyle. In the name of Jesus. ~ Amen!

Please keep journaling. Hopefully you are writing at least one sentence a day. If not…no problem. I'm not a legalist. However, I cannot express how important it is to do the work to be able to go back and see just how far God has brought you.

Days 26 – 28 (Friday – Sunday)

Reflection:

_____
_____
_____
_____
_____
_____
_____
_____
_____
_____
_____
_____
_____
_____

We are going to work through this worksheet for the next three days.

Let's Begin: What Is Your Story?

Review and write in your journal. Write your story. It can be a couple of paragraphs, but you probably need a couple of pages. Write about the weight you are experiencing (body weight and other weight such as the weight of stress, life, finances, wounds, etc.).

Get comfortable with your story. Remove the masks. This story will not be shared. It's your story for you to work through.

Here are the steps for the next three days:

1) Write your story.
2) Read Ruth 1:6-22.
3) Do the Inductive Study Method using the Ruth passage of Scripture.
4) Draw the connection of Ruth's story and your story (similarities and differences).

With this passage of Scripture, please answer these questions: Inductive Study Method (Observation, Interpretation, Application)

Observation answers the question: "What does the passage of Scripture say?" This is the foundation which must be laid first if you want to accurately interpret and have right application for God's Word. It is discovering what is being said—and this requires time and practice.

Taking time to observe Scriptures leads to correct interpretation and provides the foundation for personal application. Always begin with prayer for the Lord to open your eyes and illuminate His truth in your heart and mind through His Spirit. God provides each believer with a personal teacher in the person of the Holy Spirit, Who enlightens our minds.

1) **Observation:** What do you see? ~ Who is in the passage of Scripture? What are they saying? Where is this taking place? When is it happening? Why?

_____
_____
_____
_____
_____
_____
_____

2) **Interpretation:** What does it mean? ~ Why is he writing this? What is the culture?

_____
_____
_____
_____
_____
_____
_____

3) **Application:** How does this apply to me today? ~ Ask yourself, "So What?" What is God trying to move you to?

_____
_____
_____
_____
_____
_____
_____

Days 26 – 28 (Friday – Sunday)

Before you say it…yes, this takes work. We have to get to the root of what's going on. Don't you want to know?

Scripture: Ruth 1:6-22

When Naomi heard in Moab that the Lord had come to the aid of his people by providing food for them, she and her daughters-in-law prepared to return home from there. With her two daughters-in-law she left the place where she had been living and set out on the road that would take them back to the land of Judah. Then Naomi said to her two daughters-in-law, "Go back, each of you, to your mother's home. May the Lord show you kindness, as you have shown kindness to your dead husbands and to me. May the Lord grant that each of you will find rest in the home of another husband." Then she kissed them goodbye and they wept aloud and said to her, "We will go back with you to your people."

But Naomi said, "Return home, my daughters. Why would you come with me? Am I going to have any more sons, who could become your husbands? Return home, my daughters; I am too old to have another husband. Even if I thought there was still hope for me—even if I had a husband tonight and then gave birth to sons—would you wait until they grew up? Would you remain unmarried for them? No, my daughters. It is more bitter for me than for you, because the Lord's hand has turned against me!" At this they wept aloud again. Then Orpah kissed her mother-in-law goodbye, but Ruth clung to her.

"Look," said Naomi, "your sister-in-law is going back to her people and her gods. Go back with her." But Ruth replied, "Don't urge me to leave you or to turn back from you. Where you go I will go, and where you stay I will stay. Your people will be my people and your God my God. Where you die I will die, and there I will be buried. May the Lord deal with me, be it ever so severely, if even death separates you and me." When Naomi realized that Ruth was determined to go with her, she stopped urging her.

So the two women went on until they came to Bethlehem. When they arrived in Bethlehem, the whole town was stirred because of them, and the women exclaimed, "Can this be Naomi?"

"Don't call me Naomi," she told them. "Call me Mara, because the Almighty has made my life very bitter. I went away full, but the Lord has brought me back empty. Why call me Naomi? The Lord has afflicted me; the Almighty has brought misfortune upon me." So Naomi returned from Moab accompanied by Ruth the Moabite, her daughter-in-law, arriving in Bethlehem as the barley harvest was beginning.

Philippians 4:8

Finally, brothers and sisters, whatever is true, whatever is noble, whatever is right, whatever is pure, whatever is lovely, whatever is admirable—if anything is excellent or praiseworthy—think about such things.

_____
_____
_____
_____
_____

Prayer:

Lord, help me along this journey. It's becoming more difficult, but I want to know You and the power of Your resurrection. Jesus, give to me the strength to write my story so I may get to the root of what's going on. In the name of Jesus I pray. ~ Amen.

Ladies, I am praying for all of you as you write your story.

Week 5 ~ Day 29

Reflection:

How was your weekend? Returning to Day 25, how many negative thoughts did you have to confront?

___
___
___
___
___

It is easy to slip back to old habits and ways of thinking, but God is speaking…please listen. Some of you will begin to wonder if this is really working. Remember, you have to do the work. For others, motivation and excitement begin to disappear. The relationship with God should be growing deeper. Dig deep and experience what you did the first week when you were experiencing victory after victory. List some of your struggles:

___
___
___
___

Now that you have listed your struggles, find ways to regain your motivation to keep going. List two or three things you are going to do to keep moving forward. Remember, we are on a journey.

___
___
___
___

This is where the enemy comes in to steal, kill, and destroy, BUT Jesus comes to bring life and to bring it abundantly.

KEY: Journal! I cannot stress to you how much writing in your journal makes a difference. One sentence can make a difference. Go back to Day 1, 2, and 3 and read what you have written in your journal. It will bring life back in to what you are doing today.

This struggle is real, but we are more than conquerors through Christ who gives us strength.

Here's a testimony I received from one of the ladies in the BETA group. I pray it will motivate you.

"I got the job! After joining Getting to the Root of It: A Healing Balm of Freedom, I started doing everything God was instructing me. I am praying. I think I am listening. I am studying. I am using my journal. God told me I would receive a call, but He never told me from whom. I received a call from the HR director of the school system for an interview. After the interview I received the job offer. I know it's what I'm doing on this journey. Plus the weight on my shoulders is lifting. Thank you for doing what God has called you to do. PS. I applied for this position last year and did not get this job. This time there was something different. I felt the difference." (B. L., Pickerington, OH)

What's your testimony?

_____
_____
_____
_____
_____
_____
_____
_____

Scripture: Romans 8:31-39

More Than Conquerors

What, then, shall we say in response to these things? If God is for us, who can be against us? He who did not spare his own Son, but gave him up for us all—how will he not also, along with him, graciously give us all things? Who will bring any charge against those whom God has chosen? It is God who justifies. Who then is the one who condemns? No one. Christ Jesus who died—more than that, who was raised to life—is at the right hand of God and is also interceding for us. Who shall separate us from the love of Christ? Shall trouble or hardship or persecution or famine or nakedness or danger or sword? As it is written:

"For your sake we face death all day long;
we are considered as sheep to be slaughtered."

No, in all these things we are more than conquerors through him who loved us. For I am convinced that neither death nor life, neither angels nor demons, neither the present nor the future, nor any powers, neither height nor depth, nor anything else in all creation, will be able to separate us from the love of God that is in Christ Jesus our Lord.

Prepare:

With this passage of Scripture, please answer these questions: Inductive Study Method (Observation, Interpretation, Application)

Observation answers the question: "What does the passage of Scripture say?" This is the foundation which must be laid first if you want to accurately interpret and have right application for God's Word. It is discovering what is being said — and this requires time and practice.

Taking time to observe Scriptures leads to correct interpretation and provides the foundation for personal application. Always begin with prayer for the Lord to open your eyes and illumine His truth in your heart and mind through His Spirit. God provides each believer with a personal teacher in the person of the Holy Spirit, Who enlightens our minds.

1) **Observation:** What do you see? ~ Who is in the passage of Scripture? What are they saying? Where is this taking place? When is it happening? Why?

_____
_____
_____
_____
_____
_____
_____
_____
_____
_____
_____
_____
_____
_____

2) **Interpretation:** What does it mean? ~ Why is he writing this? What is the culture?

_____
_____
_____
_____
_____
_____
_____
_____
_____
_____

3) **Application:** How does this apply to me today? ~ Ask yourself, "So what?" What is God trying to move you to?

_____
_____
_____
_____
_____
_____
_____
_____
_____
_____
_____
_____
_____

Scripture: Philippians 4:8

Finally, brothers and sisters, whatever is true, whatever is noble, whatever is right, whatever is pure, whatever is lovely, whatever is admirable—if anything is excellent or praiseworthy—think about such things.

Prayer:

May God reveal to me great and mighty things today. ~ Amen.

Days 30 and 31

Reflection:
_____
_____
_____
_____
_____
_____

Identifying triggers. Journaling is going to be very important moving forward. Things may become a little more difficult, but with Christ we are victorious!

I will use having migraines as an example of triggers.

My physician tells me to keep a journal to help identify what may trigger my headaches/migraines. If I notice a trigger I am to write it down. In my journal I am to write down what I was doing, feeling, or eating in the hours before each headache. Once I have experienced a major migraine I am to share my diary/journal with my physician to help find the cause of my headaches. This helps with treatment of future headaches, follow-up care, and when to seek expert medical advice.

As we think about our relationship with food, stress, wounds, rejections, etc., with God, what are some things that draw us closer, and what are some things that may draw us away?

_____
_____
_____
_____
_____
_____

When it comes to Getting to the Root of It: A Healing Balm of Freedom, we have to pay attention to what seems to trigger our eating habits, our lack of exercise, our wounds and rejections triggers, our stress triggers, etc. Once identified we are to try and deal with the triggers when we can by trying to identify the cause. With God as our Father we are to simply turn them over to Him. Through it all we are encouraged to keep a diary/journal. Write down what is going on when you are triggered to eat or do things that God is directing you away from, and to write down what you are feeling when you are pulled to eat things that may not be the things God will have you to eat…along with identifying what you are doing. For treatment you are to take it all to the Lord and leave it there.

Assignment:

Every time you eat sugar (coffee creamer, candy, cake, pies, added sugar, etc.) write it down. At the end of these two days return to your list and ask, "Why did I eat this? How do I feel now that I have consumed these food choices? Is there anything I could have eaten instead?"

Scripture: John 6:35

> Then Jesus declared, "I am the bread of life. Whoever comes to me will never go hungry, and whoever believes in me will never be thirsty."

Philippians 4:8

> Finally, brothers and sisters, whatever is true, whatever is noble, whatever is right, whatever is pure, whatever is lovely, whatever is admirable—if anything is excellent or praiseworthy—think about such things.

Prayer:

> God, I need Your strength. Help me to identify what triggers my life response or lack of response. Help me identify the triggers that lead me to food or other things. In the name of Jesus. ~ Amen.

Day 32

Reflection:

Write your vision. Make it plain. Be sure you continue to journal.

_____
_____
_____
_____
_____
_____
_____
_____
_____
_____
_____
_____

Water. Water. Water. You should have a goal to drink half your body weight in water. When we drink LIVING WATER (prayer and Scripture) we are partaking of Jesus and HIs Word. Additionally, I am encouraging all of us to drink half our body weight in water. Half our body weight in water is taking your weight and dividing it by half. That is what you drink in ounces. I also want us to look at this as a tithe and an offering. That means to strive to drink another 10 ounces as your offering over and above your tithe of drinking half your body weight in ounces.

Remember, I am NOT a dietitian, physician, or nutritionist. I am a child of God who has answered a call from God to develop prayer strategies to set women free from the weight of life.

Let's talk about avoidance. Read the following blog post and then write about your wounds: https://gaildudley.wordpress.com/2017/03/13/surrender-let-the-holy-spirit-guide-you/.

I hear the Lord calling us to stop avoiding the inevitable. Inevitable means: Incapable of being avoided or prevented. We must start looking at ourselves in an authentic view. Don't hate me. Take a picture of yourself in a swimsuit. Post it in your closet, on your bathroom mirror, on your treadmill, etc. Post wherever you will see it daily. This is the real you! In your journal write down what you see.

When you have a moment read this blog post: https://gaildudley.wordpress.com/2017/03/14/pray-to-lose-is-saving-my-life-right-now

I will never forget the time when I noticed my rear end as I passed by a mirror in Nordstrom Rack. I thought, "That's disgusting." Wrong word choice. God made me. I am not disgusting. So I have had to deal with my thoughts of myself now that I have visually seen myself in an authentic view. I cannot ignore what I saw. I have to be authentic and deal with it.

In your journal write the time you noticed something about yourself that did not sit well with you. Yes, it's getting tough.

Remember, tomorrow will be a day of fasting. Please prepare now to do a liquid-only fast on Wednesday if you are able to do so from 8:00 a.m. until 6:00 p.m.

Journal ladies. We must journal.

Scripture: You pick a new one to use both Tuesday and Wednesday.

Philippians 4:8

> Finally, brothers and sisters, whatever is true, whatever is noble, whatever is right, whatever is pure, whatever is lovely, whatever is admirable — if anything is excellent or praiseworthy — think about such things.

Prayer:

> Lord, it's getting more and more difficult, but I trust You! Encourage me, Lord. Hear my prayers. ~ Amen.

Days 33 – 35 (Friday – Sunday)

Reflection:

Days of reading, reflecting, and journaling as the Holy Spirit leads.

Scripture: Return to reading the Ruth chapters 1 and 2 (from days 26, 27, and 28) and Philippians 4:8.

Prepare:

What masks need removing?

_____
_____
_____
_____
_____
_____
_____
_____
_____
_____
_____
_____
_____
_____
_____
_____
_____
_____
_____
_____
_____
_____
_____
_____
_____
_____

Prayer:

Lord, may we rest in Your glory as we walk this journey each day. ~ Amen

Week 6 ~ Day 36

Reflection:

Review the prayer positions. Identify those positions that were comfortable and those that were not so comfortable.

_____
_____
_____
_____
_____
_____
_____
_____
_____
_____
_____
_____
_____
_____
_____
_____

This is the day we laugh and eat chocolate!

Truth: it is wonderful to laugh! Ever notice how attitudes change when we chuckle or burst into laughter? The atmosphere shifts when we laugh. People around us will laugh when we laugh. Ever notice that? A weight is lifted when we laugh, even if it is temporary. Let's agree that something happens when we laugh. Studies have shown that laughter increases dopamine, which is the pleasure chemical messenger in the brain. Even our lungs actually work out, so to speak, when we have a deep belly laugh, which provides more oxygen for the body. Laughing helps work out your abs, and to some degree increases your tolerance for pain. Yes…from laughing.

Chocolate. Dark chocolate, that is…can diminish pain. Physicians have determined antioxidants found in dark chocolate contain over 60 percent or more cocoa. There is medical research that concludes that eating dark chocolate can help with high blood pressure and heart disease. **(Please check with your physician before taking on chocolate for these or other medical conditions.)**

Let's fill our day with some laughter and dark chocolate!

Question: How often do you laugh each day? Each week? _____

Exercise:

1) Make it a point to laugh at yourself. In your journal write down the incident that caused you to laugh and include what it felt like to laugh in that moment.

2) Intentionally watch a sitcom or a cartoon that makes you laugh. Think about why the actors or lines in the sitcom bring you to laugh.

3) Intentionally read the comics in the newspaper. What makes you laugh about the comics?

4) Find old images of you in high school or at a family reunion at a young age. What is it about the images that brings you to laughter?

5) Notice your attitude and your decrease of stress throughout the day as you laugh. Journal about it.

Scripture: Psalm 126:1-3

When the Lord restored the fortunes of Zion, we were like those who dreamed. Our mouths were filled with laughter, our tongues with songs of joy. Then it was said among the nations, "The Lord has done great things for them." The Lord has done great things for us, and we are filled with joy.

Ecclesiastes 3:4

…a time to weep and a time to laugh, a time to mourn and a time to dance…

Prayer:

Lord, fill me with joy and laughter. I wouldn't mind some chocolate too. ~ Amen.

Day 37

A day of rest. Use this space to draw, doodle, and color.

Just Doodle

Day 38

Reflection:

Write as God speaks.

_____
_____
_____
_____
_____
_____
_____
_____
_____
_____

This is a day of fast. Allow God to move.

Make this a day of prayer. Fast. Pray. Listen. Journal.

We are all different. Have you noticed how some diets will work for some and not for others? That's because we are different. This journey is designed with each individual person in mind. The goal is to lay aside the weight—*all* the weight.

Today is also a day to <u>organize</u> as you fast. Marcia Ramsland, author of *Simplify Your Life*, uses the acronym PUSH to help women simplify their lives.

P is for Project—A one-time focused investment to simplify an area of life
U is for You—You've got to organize in a way that makes sense to you
S is for System—Create a dependable plan that maintains the project you just completed
H is for Habit—A valuable personal daily routine to stay organized[4]

---

[4] Marcia Ramsland, *Simplify Your Life: Get Organized and Stay that Way* (Nashville, TN: W Publishing Group, Thomas Nelson, 2003), 6.

What do you need to get organized?

___

Prepare:

Write down your areas of struggle.

___

Write your areas of strength.

___

Drink your water! Drink your water!
Half your body weight in ounces.

Scripture: Choose a Scripture to meditate on throughout the day.

Philippians 4:8

> Finally, brothers and sisters, whatever is true, whatever is noble, whatever is right, whatever is pure, whatever is lovely, whatever is admirable—if anything is excellent or praiseworthy—think about such things.

Prayer:

> God, (you talk with Him). This is your prayer time.

Day 39

Reflection:

How was your day of fasting and drinking half your body weight in water? Write your progress with water. Did you come close to half your weight in ounces? Did you drink three glasses? Did you get one sip in? That's great! We must start somewhere.

_____
_____
_____
_____
_____
_____
_____
_____
_____
_____

Time to go deeper. We may wrestle with God on this one, but we have to deal with every area.

Some of us eat and/or drink out of our emotions. Emotional eating/drinking comes from our trying to mask something that we do not wish to deal with.

Please pray and then take some time to read through the blog post (link below) written by my friend, Tina. She shares herself and how she drank wine to mask the pain. For some it may be wine, and for others it may be snack foods or lack of food with nutritional value, and yet for others it may be something totally different. Regardless of what… this article will help us begin to process why we do what we do. If nothing more, it may reveal a mask.

We are talking about addictions. When we deal with the weight of life, we can become addicted as well as attached to our addictions. Being attached to our addictions allows us to mask the pain.

Time to pull back another layer. Please read the article and then write down your emotions after reading the article in your journal. How do you mask pain?

Here's the article link:
http://www.tinaosterhouse.com/when-alcohol-isnt-your-best-friend-anymore

Scripture: Romans 12:1-2

Therefore, I urge you, brothers and sisters, in view of God's mercy, to offer your bodies as a living sacrifice, holy and pleasing to God—this is your true and proper worship. Do not conform to the pattern of this world, but be transformed by the renewing of your mind. Then you will be able to test and approve what God's will is—his good, pleasing and perfect will.

Ephesians 6:12

For our struggle is not against flesh and blood, but against the rulers, against the authorities, against the powers of this dark world and against the spiritual forces of evil in the heavenly realms.

Philippians 4:8

Finally, brothers and sisters, whatever is true, whatever is noble, whatever is right, whatever is pure, whatever is lovely, whatever is admirable—if anything is excellent or praiseworthy—think about such things.

Prayer:

Lord, help me. Lord, I know that my struggle is not against flesh and blood, but against the rulers, against the authorities, against the powers of this dark world and against the spiritual forces of evil in the heavenly realms. Lord, hear my prayers and show me Your grace and mercy. Father, remove the tastes of the very things You do not want for me to partake in. In the name of Jesus I pray. ~ Amen.

Ladies, we can do this!

Days 40 – 42 (Friday – Sunday)

Reflection:

What's working for you? Where do you struggle?

_____
_____
_____
_____
_____
_____
_____
_____
_____

The next three days we will focus on our food intake. We did a similar exercise a couple weeks ago. This week we are taking steps to record our meals.

1) Write down everything you eat for breakfast, lunch, dinner, and snacks.

2) Write down everything you drink to include coffee, tea, and water.

3) Write down how you feel after writing down your meals.

We are attacking our emotions to our food intake. What are your immediate emotions when you think about recording your feed intake?

_____
_____
_____
_____
_____
_____

Scripture for this exercise: 1 Corinthians 6:19-20 (Study daily.)

> Do you not know that your bodies are temples of the Holy Spirit, who is in you, whom you have received from God? You are not your own; you were bought at a price. Therefore honor God with your bodies.

What are the Scriptures saying?
What is the observation?
What is the interpretation?
What is the application?
How will you apply this Scripture each day of this week to your daily life?

Scripture: Philippians 4:8

> Finally, brothers and sisters, whatever is true, whatever is noble, whatever is right, whatever is pure, whatever is lovely, whatever is admirable—if anything is excellent or praiseworthy—think about such things.

Prepare:

Before you begin this exercise, how will you prepare? Fitness Pal App may be something to add to your smartphone or tablet to help you keep track, however, it's important to do this on a poster board as well.

_____
_____
_____
_____
_____
_____
_____
_____
_____
_____
_____
_____
_____
_____
_____
_____
_____
_____

Prayer:
   Lord, this is the day You have made. We choose to rejoice and be glad in it. ~ Amen.

Week 7 ~ Days 43 – 45

Reflection:
_____
_____
_____
_____
_____
_____

Day 43 ~ (Monday)

Write a couple of paragraphs and send to me about your journey at GED@MIMToday.org. What were your highs of the journey? What times of the day did you hear clearly from God? What changes in your diet have your incorporated? What changes in your mind-set? What new exercises did you begin doing? What were your struggles, etc.?

Day 44 (Tuesday)

Write a list of four hobbies that you enjoy. You can include things you want to learn in the future. Then take out your calendar and schedule in time for one of the hobbies listed. For example, if you wrote cycling, put a bike ride into your schedule in the next week. If you like cooking, sign up for a cooking class or buy yourself a new cookbook and try a few new recipes this week. What do you want to do for you?

Day 45 (Wednesday)

The day of fasting and prayer.

Revisit the seven prayer positions and take time to pray in each position throughout the day. Also reread Isaiah 58. Study throughout the day by breaking up the chapter. Verses 1-3 in the morning, 4-6 in the afternoon, and 7-14 in the evening. Write down what God is speaking.

Prepare:

Write down your areas of struggle.

_____
_____
_____
_____
_____
_____
_____
_____
_____

Write your areas of strength.

_____
_____
_____
_____
_____
_____
_____
_____
_____
_____

You have four more days to go. READY?

Scripture: Foundational Scripture – Philippians 4:8

> Finally, brothers and sisters, whatever is true, whatever is noble, whatever is right, whatever is pure, whatever is lovely, whatever is admirable—if anything is excellent or praiseworthy—think about such things.

Prayer:

> Lord, we want to hear from You greater and more clearly than ever before. God, bless our journey and help us get to the root of it all. We desire to live in Your abundance. We focus on having faith enough for this day. In the name of Jesus we pray. ~ Amen!

Days 46 - 47

Reflection:

Faith. Surrender. Know Him (a refresher from Days 12-14).

_____
_____
_____
_____
_____
_____
_____
_____
_____
_____
_____
_____
_____

You are at the end of this journey. Some may have experienced progress. Some may have experienced much success. Others may still be struggling and questioning. Here's a message: "Do not give up! Do not throw in the towel. You can always start over and hit repeat."

Anything we do in life is a process. This journey is a process.

This journey can make a difference in our lives. Some are saying that they are not losing a bunch of weight, but they are witnessing their clothes loosening, the minds clearer, and a growing intimate relationship with Jesus. In the BETA group, one lady stated that she no longer feels like a victim consumed in bondage since Getting to the Root of It: A Healing Balm of Freedom. Another lady shared that she has deep wounds and she wants to be free. She started sharing how she has masked her wounds with pills, alcohol, and sex, and how she wants to join this journey to be freed.

God is saying, "You are just where I need you."

The first time through you may not have completed each assignment. Do yourself a favor and start with Day 1 and be sure to complete assignments. No guilt and no shame. This entire process is between you and God. The goal is to lose the weight of life off of your shoulders with a possible benefit of seeing loss in body weight.

Hard word: Stop pretending and lose the masks. Time to get to the root of it. To do so I have taken a chapter from my book *Ready to Change My Name: A Spiritual Journey from Fear to Faith* to share with all of you. (Chapter included on page 127. You may order the book at www.GailDudley.com if interested.)

Prepare:

Write down your areas of struggle when it comes to your masks (if you have any) and addictions.

_____
_____
_____
_____
_____
_____

Write your areas of strength (masks and addictions if you have any).

_____
_____
_____
_____
_____
_____

Scripture: Read Ruth chapters 1 and 2.

Philippians 4:8

> Finally, brothers and sisters, whatever is true, whatever is noble, whatever is right, whatever is pure, whatever is lovely, whatever is admirable—if anything is excellent or praiseworthy—think about such things.

Prayer:

> Lord, I love You! I avail my life to You. Although this will be painful, help me remove masks and free me from my addictions. In the name of Jesus. Amen! ~ Amen.

Day 48

Reflection:
_____
_____
_____
_____
_____
_____
_____
_____

We are at the end of this journey.

Please take this day to go through and reflect over the past 48 days. Write in your journal your reflections.

1) Review your two-column exercise where you drew the lines from food items to names and conflict. If you were to complete that exercise again, would anything change?

2) Has your mind-set changed from your list of negativities? Is that list decreasing? How are you handing the negatives in your life since this journey?

3) Drinking half your body weight in ounces of water. How close did you come to the goal? Did you exceed your goal?

4) Journaling. Take time today to read through your journal. Jot down your thoughts today.

5) Go through your prayer jar. How many prayers were answered?

6) Do you have your faith portrait positioned so you can see it each day? Can you see your faith in action?

7) Did you receive clarity during fasting days? If so how will you implement fasting into your lifestyle? Will you continue a day of fasting? Explain. What were the benefits of fasting?

8) Prayer positions. How often are you using the different positions when you pray? Have you noticed a change in your prayer life? Explain.

9) Think about the masks you previously juggled, and maybe still juggle. What's the pain you experience while wearing the masks? How will you remove all masks going forward?

10) Food addictions. How are you dealing with any you may have?

11) Inductive Study Method of studying the Bible. How are you doing with going through God's Word and using this method?

12) How will you remain in alignment with God? What are some daily practices you will implement?

13) Obedience. Remembering 2 Kings 4:1-7...are you being obedient to God's instructions?

14) Remembering the 3 Cs. How's your spirit? Have you dealt with "Critical. Comparing. and/or Controlling Spirit"?

15) How are you living out your authentic self?

Yes, we did a lot during this journey. This is only the beginning. We may have conquered many challenges, and we are victorious. AND...we must continue the journey of complete freedom in Christ. How will you live free moving forward?

My encouragement to you would be to go back through each day over the last seven weeks. What do you need to focus on?

Scripture: Philippians 4:8

Finally, brothers and sisters, whatever is true, whatever is noble, whatever is right, whatever is pure, whatever is lovely, whatever is admirable—if anything is excellent or praiseworthy—think about such things.

Prayer:

Thy will be done! ~ Amen.

Sunday ~ Day 49 – It's a Celebration!

CONGRATULATIONS!
7 WEEKS … 49 DAYS COMPLETED

———————————— ✴ ————————————

You made a committment to Get to the Root and lay aside the weight of life.

Celebrate Success!

———————————— ✴ ————————————

WHAT'S NEXT?

Take the pledge. I, _____, will commit to _____ _____ _____ as I continue this journey.

Just Doodle

SUPPLEMENTAL ARTICLE FROM *READY TO CHANGE MY NAME*
BY GAIL DUDLEY, COPYRIGHT © 2012

REMOVAL OF THE MASKS

Real or phony? That is the question. Can we talk? I mean really talk? I would like for us to have the kind of conversation that is without the make-up, dress-up, use of proper words and such. It's just you and me letting our hair down and being real for a moment. Forget about who is watching or who we need to impress. Let's take off the mask and become upfront and personal and get to the real issues that we face in our lives about ourselves.

Allow yourself to move out of your comfort zone and think about the real you. Who are you? Take your time and get acquainted with you. I realize that this may be difficult so allow me to help you take the necessary steps to survive the big question: Who are you? Are you real or phony? No one has to know your answer but you. Be still for a moment and reflect on exactly who you are. Forget about your demanding boss, coworkers, friends, and family. Yes, everyone wants something from you and they want it right now! But do not worry yourself with them right now. I am asking you to think about *you* for a moment.

Ever found it difficult to get in tune with you? If so, close your eyes and dream of a more peaceful place—a place of crystal clear waters, beautiful sunrises, and breathtaking sunsets—a place where you can meet Jesus. A "safe place"; a place of letting go and allowing God to lead, guide, and direct you; a place in which you do not feel the pressure to do something outstanding, important, or fantastic for people to like, validate, or agree with. Enter into that safe place where you can be vulnerable and securely share with Jesus what you are experiencing. Tell Him your hurt, fears, and the areas where you may need inner healing. So often there are many of us who seek approval from others. After all, we reason, who could possibly like me for just being me? We repeatedly feel we need to do something more, so others will approve of us and love us. Everywhere we turn, we are faced with pleas for help. Our spouse, our boss, our children, our friends, our family, our elderly relatives all cry out for our time and attention, wanting us to do things their way, all based upon their approval. In your safe place with Jesus you will not have to experience any of those requests. Take time with Jesus and steal away into a resting place of peace and freedom.

Requests continue to stack up, demanding our attention. It is too difficult to say no, the guilt is too great. We fear that we may lose something or someone if we go against their request. So-called urgent demands are continually placed on our time and energy. Mask after mask we change to fit with the demand. The urgent becomes a tyrant, trying to make a slave of us to the point that we never accomplish those things that are important which line up with God and His purpose for our life. We are too busy trying to be someone else that we lose sight of who we are. What can we truly accomplish trying to live the life of someone else and not our own? And if that's not enough, we have such unrealistic expectations of ourselves that we become depressed and lost. Why are we so surprised at ourselves when we get sick or become tired, ready to give up and give in? Who are we trying to impress anyway? When do we take the time and ask God if this is His plan for us?

The Bible says in Philippians 4:8, "Finally, brother, whatever is true, whatever is noble, whatever is right, whatever is pure, whatever is lovely, whatever is admirable—if anything is excellent or praiseworthy, think about such things." When truth is revealed, we have the power to decisively and courageously take off the masks. Satan has lied to us long enough! It's not about what others have to say about you—it's what *God* has to say. God's Word is truth!

The first thing that I would like to suggest would be for you to face your flesh. This can be a very painful experience but a freeing experience as well. I can remember facing myself for the first time in my mid-thirties. I had to identify with who I was and who I had become in spite of what God had created me to be. I'm reminded that God is a gentle and kind God; He won't force Himself on anyone. So He allowed me to be who I thought I wanted to be. I became negative and selfish, while spending my life trying to please others. This was not the life God had for me. But I was wearing so many masks that I didn't know which one was which. Yes, today I am free, I can talk about it now, and I want you to be free as well. I had to realize that the Creator wanted me to be who He created me to be. That meant that I had to remove all of the masks and walk in the shoes that were designed only for me. It took some pruning, cutting, and peeling to align my will with God's will. God taught me that no one needed to validate me but God Himself. What a freeing statement!

I had so many people trying to tell me who I was, what I needed, and who was the best one to do this and that for me. People would try to tell me what to wear and what I liked and didn't like. All along I knew what I wanted to wear, what I liked and disliked, and I knew what God was telling me; I just wasn't listening. I even had people telling me what was best for my husband. They would tell me what he wanted, liked, and disliked. I can remember when someone told me that I needed to minister to my husband, when I was already ministering to him. *Imagine that!* People actually became angry with me because I didn't agree with their thoughts and theories. When you go against people and take a stand for what you believe, and that belief differs from what others think you should do or say, people will begin to treat you in cruel and mean ways. I began to see sides of personalities that I didn't know existed. If you're not following God, you will get confused.

With all the masks I wore I lost sight of who God created me to be. I would wear one mask for my mother-in-law. I wanted her to like me. I wanted her to know that her son married the right women: me. I would wear a mask for my family. As I mentioned in the last chapter, I did not want them to know that the fridge was bare. I wore a mask for my husband so that he could focus on his studies and not on how I felt about not living as I had once lived. I wore masks to hide what was really going on. My friend would ask me if I needed anything and to see if all was well. Every time she would say, "Now G, if you need anything, just let me know." I would always respond with, "Girl, everything is just fine." A few of us had a saying that went like this, "If I'm lying, I will apologize." I had to apologize to her many times. It's one thing to be faithful and another to hide behind masks. As I wore those masks I realized that I was living a lie. I would change to please my mother-in-law, change to show that everything was alright with my parents, change to make my husband think that everything was okay, change to please the people around me. Living with these masks interfered with what God was doing with me. I had to remove the masks.

I'm encouraging you to remove your masks. Early in my adult life I allowed people to dictate how I lived. Unfortunately, I ended up following them and not God. This was a costly mistake, a mistake that I plead with you not to make. Could it be that I may have been insecure? Maybe. Whatever it was, it made for an open door to let my fleshly desires take over; and it also opened the window for Satan to sneak in. As a matter of fact, he didn't sneak, he walked boldly right on in. These are traps that the enemy sets for us. Beware of the traps.

Recall Orpah's dilemma. Was it possible that she was confused, seeking comfort and security in what was familiar to her? I have come to the conclusion that Orpah was a sister who may have been insecure, full of fear, scared of the unknown, double-minded, possibly stuck in her ways, jealous, self-centered, and perhaps a people pleaser. When we get to this point, it's only by the grace of God that we don't lose our mind. When you are pleasing people and juggling masks you don't know who you are from one day to the next. Am I this person today or that person? And if we read between the lines, Orpah was wearing so many masks that on the day she was traveling, being double-minded as she was, "I'm going," "I'm turning back," she didn't know which mask to wear when. She was confused just as you and I get confused sometimes. When we reach a state of confusion, we have to know that God's grace is sufficient. When we come to a roadblock in life, as we all have, or will, and we're unsure which way to turn, be assured that the only way to turn is to God. He will direct our paths. He'll tell us what to do. The time is now that we need to remove our masks and follow God. Don't wait; do it now! Remove those masks!

Orpah vanished from the Holy Scriptures and was never heard of again. Did she miss her destiny? How do we get to a place where we obey the Spirit of the living God and get away from our flesh? We must learn to boldly and courageously face our flesh and not follow our flesh. I've heard preachers say, "What is gained in the flesh must be maintained in the flesh." The dead ends, routines, ruts, mind-sets, habits, the likes of being double-minded, the need to please people, the emotional roller coasters, the conflict with self and others, the torments and self-centeredness—these issues hold our flesh in bondage. These are masks that we create.

Please realize that our greatest enemy is the flesh! Orpah's enemy, your enemy, my enemy, is our flesh! The flesh will kill, steal, and destroy. It's the enemy. We so often want to place blame on Satan. No, we need to look at ourselves. What are we doing? Our flesh creates an overwhelming sense of our own importance or greatness. Our flesh is self-seeking, rude, and cynical; it desires to ascend to the top at any cost of others, wants to make a name for itself, and will step on others to achieve that goal. Our flesh resents correction or suggestions, resents constructive criticism, seeks praise for worldly possessions, desires praise from people, feels it's important to have a particular title, an inflated public persona, improperly uses large and complex words in order to inflate its own ego, is touchy and easily offended, brags, boasts, and believes it is better than others. Here's the truth of the matter: when operating in the flesh, we fail to see our own ignorance and don't know who we are or Whose we are. In the words of Joyce Meyer, "Refuse to live in your flesh!" Flesh resists God. We must give this baggage, all this stuff, to God.

Paul pleads with us in the book of Romans to give our bodies as a living and holy sacrifice. Therefore we have to understand that in order to be transformed in the manner that is truly acceptable to God, we have to break down the walls of our inner self that remain as unredeemed, unsurrendered, unenlightened areas of our flesh. In case you're still missing the point, allow me to bring it a little closer to home. Flesh Syndrome: "You have failed to meet my needs," "You have not met my expectations," "You have not satisfied me or my desires," "You are insensitive to me," "You don't care about me," "I have to think of my happiness," "I owe it to myself," "I deserve to do this for a little while," "I have my rights," "I do not have to put up with this," "I can't take it anymore," "I'm leaving." Have you said any of these things? Go back to Orpah for a moment while she was walking the road to Bethlehem with Naomi and Ruth. At one moment, she was wearing the mask of people pleasing and yet at another moment she wanted to do her own thing. She changed her masks back and forth. She wanted to do her own thing, yet also wanted to please Naomi.

Here's a question: Could Orpah have been in competition with Ruth? Ruth is standing with Naomi. She wanted to be with her people and make Naomi's God her God. Was Orpah waiting on Ruth to make the first move? Who or what are you waiting on? Who are we seeking our approval from? The Bible says in the book of Psalms that "We are wonderfully made." We are uniquely made by God. There is no one else like you but you. **Sister, take off your mask and reveal your true self!** Again, no one has to validate us but God. God wants our obedience. He desires that we be obedient to His will and His way. Has God called you to do something, but you're not sure which mask you have on?

Because of the images we feel that we must portray, we wear masks to cover up some of these actions, not realizing that the covers must soon fall whether we want them to or not. After a while it's hard to keep up with the daily masks one wears. Just think: We wear our work mask, church mask, friendship mask, all the many relationship masks, and underneath it all is our real self. Who are you?

Will the real

_____

(put your name in the blank)

please remove your mask and become the person that God has ordained for you to be?

Let me warn you in advance. Removing your masks my cause you to lose friends and may even cause people to talk badly about you. Showing who you really are may literally change your world. But you need to know that it's okay. I'm a living witness that living according to who God created you to be is the most freeing experience that you will ever know. I have had people say to me, "What's going on with you? You never used to act like this." My response is, "There's nothing going on with me. You just have never known the real me."

I have even reintroduced myself to people. "Hello, I'm Gail E. Dudley." "I'm God's child." "I now live to please Him." If this makes people uncomfortable and they walk away from you and whatever relationship you had with them, **THAT'S THEIR PROBLEM, THEIR ISSUE, NOT YOURS!**

Let's pray.

Father, in the name of Jesus, help me to remove the masks that are hiding me from being me. Please give me the strength to be who You have created me to be. Let me realize that no one has to validate me but You, Lord.

STEPS ON THE JOURNEY

Think about the masks that you wear on a daily basis and describe how you feel about each mask.
_____
_____
_____
_____

Do you ever forget which mask you are wearing? Explain.
_____
_____
_____
_____

How many masks are you wearing?_____ Why?
_____
_____
_____
_____

As God gives you the strength to remove each mask, how do you think your life will be different? Explain.
_____
_____
_____
_____

Why do you hide behind the masks in your life?
_____
_____
_____
_____

What relationships do you believe you'll lose if you remove your mask? Explain.

_____
_____
_____
_____
_____

What's your greatest fear in the removal of each mask? Please describe in detail.

_____
_____
_____
_____
_____
_____
_____
_____
_____
_____
_____

Please Note:

**This process will not conclude overnight.
Be patient and know that God is God.**

"Your mask is hindering the real you."

About the Author

Transparent, authentic, fierce, fearless, focused, and faithful are a few words to describe Gail. Fun, loving, and outgoing are words that express her everyday experience. Gail is determined to encourage someone and motivate everyone.

Gail is committed to a calling of encouraging others and prayer. She is a blogger and the author of nine books. Additionally, Gail is the CEO and publisher of *READY Publication*, a quarterly print and digital magazine with a readership in seventeen countries. *READY Publication* is edgy, different, and content-rich, and was created to give a platform for women and girls to share their voices.

Ministry Focus:

In 2009 Gail was ordained as a pastor with a calling to train and equip the saints for the work of the ministry. This transparent vessel of God has been anointed with a spirit of intercession to pray on behalf of the saints and blessed with the gifts to teach God's people. Gail has completed eighty-five hours of "Formational Prayer" from Ashland Theological Seminary and conducts inner-healing sessions for individuals ready to be delivered from their wounds.

Advocacy Focus:

Gail Dudley is widely recognized for her contributions around advocacy and community building. A student of public administration with more than twenty-five years of leadership experience in public, corporate, nonprofit, and community contexts, Gail has demonstrated a passion for engaging the growing needs of declining neighborhoods by encouraging creative partnerships and the healthy stewardship of human, capital, and information resources. Gail is an accomplished team builder, conference and workshop speaker, and developer. A certified staff development trainer since 1994 who has received training from The Points of Light Foundation and Train the Trainer certification from the National Multicultural Institute, she has authored many training resources to support the development of volunteer groups, capital campaigns, and broad community network initiatives. She recently designed a successful civic engagement program, Politically SAVVY, which has launched hundreds of women into the meaningful work of community impact.

Five Pillars:

As a publisher, philanthropist, platform builder, political influencer, prayer missionary, and author, Gail is called upon to speak in small groups and on significant platforms as a conference and workshop speaker. Among her travels, she has been honored to speak in Canada; London, England; South Africa; and Zimbabwe, to name a few, equipping and motivating women around the world to walk boldly into their promised future. Additionally, Gail has been invited to travel the world on international missionary prayer journeys, teaching and giving prayer instructions in Herrnhut, Germany; Israel; and Greece. Gail continues to receive invitations to speak for women's retreats and conferences. Gail is the loving mother of two and married to Dr. Kevin Dudley, the senior pastor of Common Grounds Discipleship, which is not a church but a teaching ground to equip individuals for everyday living.

Follow Gail:

Twitter @GailDudley

Instagram @GailDudley

Website: www.GailDudley.com

Facebook page @GailSpeaks

READY: www.READYPublication.com

Additional Books by Gail Dudley

Who Told You That? The Truth About the Lies (book and workbook)

Transparent Moments (an eight-day devotional)

Urgent Plea for Prayer (31 days of prayer devotional)

Ready to Change My Name: A Spiritual Journey from Fear to Faith

Ready to Pray: A Spiritual Journey of Prayer and Worship (book and workbook)

READY Publication (a quarterly print and digital magazine)

www.ingramcontent.com/pod-product-compliance
Lightning Source LLC
Chambersburg PA
CBHW060301240426
43661CB00060B/2860